# Unleashing Your Authentic Self

*'Embracing divine honesty and breaking free from the flock'.*

## Wendy Sauer

# Dedication

To all those I love and all those who have struggled to be true to themselves, and to those who continue to strive for authenticity. May this book provide you with the inspiration, guidance, and support you need to embrace your true self and live your best life. This book is dedicated to you.

# Disclaimer

The information contained in this book is for general guidance and educational purposes only. It is not intended to replace professional advice or treatment. The author and publisher disclaim any liability or responsibility for any loss or damage resulting from the use of the information contained herein. Readers should consult a qualified professional for advice regarding their individual circumstances. The views and opinions expressed in this book are those of the author and do not necessarily reflect the official policy or position of any organization or entity mentioned. The author has made every effort to ensure the accuracy and completeness of the information contained in this book but cannot guarantee that all information is correct or up to date. The author and publisher reserve the right to make changes to the content of this book at any time without notice.

# Table Of Contents

# INTRODUCTION

The concept of self-authenticity is rooted in the idea of knowing oneself, which has been emphasized in various philosophical and spiritual traditions throughout history. Ancient Greek philosophers like Socrates, Plato, and Aristotle believed that self-knowledge was the key to living a fulfilling and meaningful life. They believed that true happiness and fulfillment could only be achieved by understanding oneself and one's place in the world.

In modern times, the concept of self-authenticity has gained renewed interest, as people have become more aware of the importance of living a life that is true to themselves and their values. This shift is in part due to changes in society, such as greater acceptance of diversity and individuality, as well as advancements in technology and communication that allow people to connect with others who share their values and interests.

Self-authenticity is important because it allows people to live a life that is aligned with their true selves and their values. When people are true to themselves, they are more likely to find happiness and fulfillment, and to achieve success in their personal and professional lives. This is because they are able to make choices that are in line with their goals and passions, and they are more likely to form authentic and meaningful relationships with others.

Self-authenticity involves several key components, including self-awareness, self-acceptance, and self-expression. Self-awareness involves understanding one's thoughts, feelings, and behaviours, as well as one's strengths, weaknesses, and values. Self-acceptance involves accepting oneself as one is, with all one's imperfections and flaws. Self-expression involves being true to oneself in one's actions and behaviours, and expressing one's thoughts, feelings, and beliefs in an honest and authentic way.

In order to cultivate self-authenticity, people can practice various techniques, such as self-reflection, mindfulness, and self-care. They can also seek out supportive communities and relationships that accept and encourage their authentic selves.

So how do we go about embracing our true selves? Well, it's all about acknowledging both our strengths and weaknesses, and understanding that we don't have to be perfect at everything. Instead, focus on what makes you unique and celebrate your achievements. This self-awareness will give you the confidence to trust yourself during challenging times and help you discover your passions.

Being true to yourself also enhances your decision-making abilities in all aspects of your life. When making choices that will positively impact your journey, it's crucial to align with your authentic self, rather than what others think is best for you. Remember, the only approval you need is your own.

In a nutshell, living a purposeful life is all about embracing self-honesty. By welcoming both accomplishments and disappointments with understanding, you'll not only make the most of your journey but also find joy in the experience.

In this book, I'm going to share some insights on self-authenticity - how it works, why it's so powerful, and how we can nurture more of it in our lives. So, let's dive in and uncover the incredible power of being true to ourselves!

# Chapter One

## SELF-AUTHENTICITY: WHAT IS IT?

**Unleashing the Power of Self-Authenticity**

Self-authenticity refers to the ability to stay true to oneself, to express one's true thoughts, feelings, and behaviours, and to act in accordance with one's core values and beliefs. It involves a deep sense of self-awareness, self-acceptance, and self-expression, and it can be a powerful force for personal growth, happiness, and success.

So, why is self-authenticity so important? Well, for one, it allows us to live a life that is true to ourselves, rather than one that is based on other people's expectations, beliefs, or desires. It helps us to build authentic and meaningful relationships with others, and to connect with them on a deeper level. It also enables us to make choices that are aligned with our goals, values, and passions, and to pursue a life that is fulfilling and satisfying.

However, being self-authentic can be challenging, especially in a society that often values conformity, social approval, and external validation. Many of us learn to suppress our true thoughts, feelings, and behaviours, and to present a false self to others in order to fit in, avoid conflict, or gain approval. This can lead to feelings of disconnection, dissatisfaction, and anxiety, and can prevent us from reaching our full potential.

So, how can we unleash the power of self-authenticity? Here are a few tips:

1.  Cultivate self-awareness: The first step towards self-authenticity is to develop a deep understanding of yourself - your values, beliefs, strengths, weaknesses, passions, and goals. Take time to reflect on your experiences, thoughts, and feelings, and pay attention to the things that make you feel alive, fulfilled, and authentic.

2.  Practice self-acceptance: Accepting yourself as you are - with all your flaws, imperfections, and quirks - is essential to living an authentic life. Stop comparing yourself to others and stop judging yourself harshly for your mistakes or shortcomings. Instead, focus on your strengths, and learn to love and accept yourself unconditionally.

3.  Express yourself authentically: Once you have a clear understanding of yourself, it's time to start expressing yourself authentically. Speak your truth, even if it's unpopular or goes against the grain. Share your thoughts and feelings honestly, and don't be afraid to be vulnerable or imperfect. Be true to yourself in your actions, and don't compromise your values or beliefs to please others.

4.  Build authentic relationships: Authenticity is essential to building deep and meaningful relationships with others. Seek out people who accept and appreciate you for who you are and avoid those who try to change or control you. Be honest, open, and vulnerable in your interactions with others, and listen deeply to what they have to say.

5.  Embrace your uniqueness: Finally, embrace your uniqueness and celebrate your individuality. Don't try to fit in or be like everyone else - instead, embrace your quirks, passions, and talents, and use them to make a positive impact in the world. Recognize that your authenticity is what makes you special, and that it has the power to inspire and uplift others.

Self-authenticity is a powerful force that can help us to live a life that is true to ourselves, and to achieve greater happiness, success, and fulfillment. By cultivating self-awareness, practicing self-acceptance, expressing ourselves authentically, building authentic relationships, and embracing our uniqueness, we can unleash the power of self-authenticity and live a life that is truly our own.

## Why Is Being Authentic Important?

Being authentic as stated previously, is important for several reasons:

1. It promotes self-awareness: When you are authentic, you are honest about your thoughts, feelings, and actions. This honesty leads to a deeper understanding of yourself, your strengths, your weaknesses, and your values. When you know who you are, you can make better decisions about your life, and you are more likely to find happiness and fulfillment.

2. It builds trust: When you are authentic, people trust you because they know that you are being honest and sincere. This trust can lead to deeper and more meaningful relationships, both personally and professionally.

3. It promotes growth: When you are authentic, you are open to feedback and criticism. You are willing to acknowledge your mistakes and learn from them. This mindset promotes personal and professional growth and allows you to improve yourself and your relationships with others.

4. It reduces stress and anxiety: When you are authentic, you don't have to pretend to be someone you're not. This reduces stress and anxiety because you don't have to constantly worry about maintaining a false image or hiding your true self.

5. It allows you to be happy: When you are authentic, you are true to yourself and your values. This leads to a sense of inner peace and happiness because you are living a life that is aligned with your true self.

Being authentic is important because it promotes self-awareness, builds trust, promotes growth, reduces stress and anxiety, and allows you to be happy. It enables you to live a life that is true to yourself and your values, which is essential for personal and professional success and fulfillment.

## Differentiating between self-authenticity and related concepts

---

Differentiating between self-authenticity and related concepts The degree to which someone behaves in a way that is congruent with their real ideas, values, and personality traits is referred to as self-authenticity. It entails being true to oneself and leading a life that is consistent with one's deepest hopes and desires. Self-authenticity is frequently mistaken with a number of related ideas, such as self-esteem, self-concept, and self-awareness.

An overview of how these ideas differ from self-authenticity is given below:

- Self-esteem: Self-esteem is a person's general perception of their own value and worth. It is influenced by a number of things, such as one's successes, connections, and social standing. Self-authenticity is similar to self-esteem in that it entails appreciating oneself, but it is more concerned with being genuine to oneself than with seeking praise from others.

- Self-concept: A person's perception of oneself, including their beliefs, attitudes, and values, is referred to as their self-concept. Self-concept is a more generic phrase that incorporates one's views about oneself generally, whereas self-authenticity is connected to self-concept in that it entails being true to one's beliefs and ideals.

- Self-awareness: The capacity to recognize one's own feelings, ideas, and actions is referred to as self-awareness. While self-authenticity and self-awareness are similar in that both require knowing one's deepest objectives and goals, self-awareness is a larger phrase that covers a wider variety of mental and emotional functions.

- Self-acceptance: The capacity to embrace oneself, warts, and all, is referred to as self-acceptance. While being true to oneself is a necessary component of self-authenticity, it doesn't entail accepting every element of oneself. For instance, a person who is honest may make an effort to better themselves in areas where they believe they fall short, even if that necessitates recognizing and addressing their imperfections.

- Self-actualization: The process of realizing one's full potential as a human is referred to as self-actualization. While necessary for self-actualization, self-authenticity is not the same as it. Self-authenticity is being true to oneself and leading a life that is in line with one's deepest ambitions and aspirations, whereas self-actualization entails using one's skills and abilities to accomplish meaningful goals and have a beneficial impact on the world.

- Self-transcendence: The capacity to connect with something bigger than oneself, such as a higher power, nature, or humanity as a whole, is referred to as self-transcendence. While being genuine to oneself is a requirement for self-authenticity, transcending oneself is not always necessary. On the other hand, some people could discover that leading a genuine life makes them feel more a part of something bigger than themselves.

- Self-confidence: A person who has self-confidence believes in their own skills, traits, and judgment. While self-authenticity and self-confidence are connected in that both include appreciating oneself, the former is more concerned with a person's faith in their own skills and performance. Contrarily, self-authenticity emphasizes a person's core aims, values, and desires rather than their outward performance or skills.

- Self-compassion: When faced with difficulties or failures on the personal level, self-compassion means treating oneself with kindness, care, and understanding. While being genuine to oneself is a necessary component of self-authenticity, self-compassion is not a prerequisite. When they fall short of their own expectations, some people who are sincere may be self-critical or harsh with themselves.

- Self-identity: Self-identity is a person's perception of who they are, influenced by a variety of social and personal characteristics like gender, race, culture, and religion. Self-identification and self-authenticity are connected in that both entails being genuine to oneself, while self-identity is primarily concerned with a person's social and cultural identity. On the other hand, self-authenticity is more concerned with a person's deepest aspirations, values, and desires.

- Self-expression: Self-expression is the capacity to convey one's ideas, emotions, and thoughts in a genuine and truthful way to oneself. Self-expression and self-authenticity are similar in that both entails being genuine to oneself, but self-expression is primarily concerned with sharing one's inner experiences with others. Contrarily, self-authenticity is more concerned with a person's deepest aspirations, values, and desires.

While self-authenticity is closely related to these concepts, they differ in their focus and scope. Self-esteem, self-concept, and self-confidence are more about a person's perceptions and evaluations of themselves, while self-actualization, self-transcendence, and self-expression are more about a person's pursuits and activities. Self-awareness and self-acceptance are more about a person's internal processes and attitudes towards themselves. However, all of these concepts can play a role in a person's ability to be authentic to themselves.

**Developing Self Authenticity**

Are you looking to develop your self-authenticity? Well, the good news is that it's totally possible! It just takes some introspection and determination to be true to yourself in all aspects of your life. Here are some tips to help you cultivate your self-authenticity:

First and foremost, it's important to understand who you are as a person. Take some time to think about your beliefs, values, strengths, weaknesses, passions, and goals. The more you understand yourself, the easier it will be to stay true to who you are.

It's also crucial to be honest with yourself. This means acknowledging your flaws and weaknesses without judgment. It's all about being sincere in your thoughts, feelings, and actions.

Don't be afraid to embrace your uniqueness! Instead of trying to fit into someone else's mold, take pride in your individuality and what sets you apart from others.

Setting boundaries is also key to maintaining authenticity. If something doesn't align with your values or priorities, don't hesitate to say no, and set clear limits with others.

Taking care of yourself both physically and mentally is also important in staying true to yourself. Make time for things that make you happy and prioritize your health.

Remember that authenticity is a lifelong journey of self-discovery and growth. Be open to learning new things and trying new experiences.

Practicing mindfulness techniques can also help you stay present and aware of your thoughts and feelings.

Surrounding yourself with a supportive community can also make a huge difference in staying authentic. Find people who will encourage and inspire you to stay true to yourself.

Reflecting on your experiences can also provide valuable insights into your feelings, thoughts, and actions.

Taking responsibility for your actions is also a key aspect of authenticity. Acknowledging your mistakes and making amends when necessary is a sign of integrity.

And last but not least, avoid comparing yourself to others. Everyone's path to authenticity is unique, so embrace your own journey and express yourself creatively in a way that feels authentic to you. Being vulnerable can be an important part of being authentic. It can be scary to share your true thoughts and emotions with others, but it can also lead to deeper connections and understanding. Another way to foster authenticity is to practice mindfulness. Taking the time to be present in the moment and observe your thoughts and emotions can help you become more self-aware and in tune with your true self.

 Surrounding yourself with supportive and accepting people can also make it easier to be authentic. Having a safe space to be yourself without fear of judgment can be incredibly freeing. Remember that authenticity is a process, not a destination. It takes time and effort to truly understand and embrace your true self, but the rewards are worth it. Finally, don't be afraid to seek support or guidance from a therapist or counsellor if you're struggling with authenticity. They can provide helpful tools and perspectives to guide you on your journey.

# Chapter Two

## CHALLENGES TO BEING AUTHENTIC

**The Difficulties Affecting Self-Authenticity.**

So you are interested in self-authenticity but are you struggling with some difficulties? No worries, it is completely normal! Here are some common obstacles that can get in the way of being true to yourself and how to overcome them:

Feeling like you don't fit in or being stuck in a rut can make it difficult to embrace your true self. But don't worry, you don't have to go through this alone. Reach out to friends or family members for support or consider seeking professional guidance if needed.

One of the biggest challenges to self-authenticity is having an honest conversation with yourself. This means taking the time to understand what's holding you back from being your authentic self and why. It might be difficult or uncomfortable, but confronting these issues head-on is crucial for personal growth and development.

Another key to self-authenticity is understanding your own values and beliefs. This can help you make decisions that align with your true self, rather than just following what's rational. Spend time reflecting on what's important to you in your relationships, career, and overall life. And don't forget to prioritize your physical and mental health, as well as the things that bring you joy and fulfillment.

Building meaningful relationships with others is also essential for self-authenticity. Nurture these connections by having open and honest conversations, and don't be afraid to express your true emotions. It's important to set boundaries when necessary and stand up for yourself, even if it's uncomfortable.

Remember, becoming your most authentic self is a journey, and it's okay to face obstacles along the way. With self-reflection, support, and a willingness to confront challenges head-on, you can overcome these difficulties and live a more authentic life. Good luck!

## Obstacles To Authenticity

---

Have you ever felt like you have to conform to societal expectations just to be accepted? It can be tough to be true to yourself when you feel like you're falling short of what society deems "acceptable." This is where social pressure and expectations come in, and they can have a huge impact on your ability to be authentic.

When we talk about being authentic, we mean being genuine to yourself and acting in accordance with your own principles, views, and interests. However, social pressure and expectations can make it difficult to do so. They can create a sense of conformity and self-doubt, causing you to question your skills and decisions.

Society has certain expectations for conduct, appearance, and lifestyle, which can put pressure on you to conform in order to be accepted by others. This can lead you to hide your true self and adopt attitudes and behaviours that don't align with who you really are, ultimately affecting your self-confidence.

In addition, cultural expectations can breed comparison and competition, especially with the rise of social media. It's become common to present a flawless image of yourself that adheres to cultural norms, but this can cause stress and pressure to live up to unrealistic expectations.

Finally, the fear of criticism and rejection from others can also prevent you from being authentic. You may feel like you have to conceal or suppress your true self in order to fit in and avoid negative feedback.

Social pressure and expectations in society can make it a challenge to be authentic. They create pressure to conform, instil comparison and competition, and generate a fear of judgment and rejection. It's important to be aware of these pressures and work towards embracing your true self, even in the face of societal expectations.

Are you ever worried about living up to society's expectations? It can be tough to be true to yourself when you feel like you're not meeting the standards that society deems "acceptable."

This is where social pressure and expectations come in and can have a huge impact on your ability to be authentic. Self-authenticity refers to being genuine to yourself, acting in accordance with your own principles, views, and interests, and expressing yourself without inhibition. Unfortunately, social pressure and expectations can severely hamper your ability to do so.

Society has certain expectations for conduct, appearance, and lifestyle, which can create pressure to conform to these norms to be accepted and validated by others. This can lead you to hide your true self and adopt attitudes and behaviours that don't align with who you really are, ultimately affecting your self-confidence.

Furthermore, cultural expectations can foster a sense of comparison and rivalry, especially with the rise of social media. The need to present a flawless self-image that adheres to cultural norms can cause stress and pressure to live up to unrealistic expectations. This can make you feel like you must project an untrue representation of who you are, which can further impact your self-authenticity.

The fear of criticism and rejection from others can also prevent you from being authentic. You may feel like you have to conceal or suppress your true self in order to fit in and avoid negative feedback. This can lead to a lack of self-confidence and self-expression.

It's important to be aware of these pressures and work towards embracing your true self, even in the face of societal expectations. Remember, it's okay to be different and true to yourself!

**The Way Forward.**

Are you struggling to balance your sense of self-authenticity with the pressures of society? It's definitely a tough task, but there are some tactics that you can use to stay true to yourself while navigating social expectations and pressures.

First and foremost, it's important to determine your core principles and beliefs. By understanding what you value, you can use these as a compass to guide your decision-making and remain true to yourself. Make a list of your values and beliefs and refer to it whenever you need to make a tough choice.

Surrounding yourself with supportive and accepting people can also be helpful. Seek out individuals who accept you for who you are and encourage your authenticity. This can boost your self-confidence and make it easier to express your true self.

It's important to question societal expectations and norms as well. Just because something is expected of you doesn't mean it's what's best for you. Analyse these assumptions and make decisions that align with your values and beliefs to challenge them.

Remember that no one is perfect and it's okay to accept yourself for who you are. Practice self-acceptance and self-compassion, even when you make mistakes or encounter difficulties.

Self-reflection is also key. Take time to consider your thoughts, feelings, and actions regularly. This can help increase your self-awareness and allow you to spot when you're not being true to yourself. Use this information to adjust your actions and beliefs to better align with your genuine self.

Don't be afraid to seek professional assistance if you're having trouble balancing your sense of self-authenticity with the demands of society. A therapist or counsellor can provide you with the tools and techniques you need to overcome these obstacles and develop a more authentic self.

Remember, it's possible to be true to yourself while also navigating the pressures of society. Use these tactics to stay true to who you are and live your best life!

**Here are a few tactics that I found to be useful:**

- Determine your core principles and beliefs: Being aware of your principles and beliefs will help you stay true to your true self. Create a list of your values and beliefs and use it as a compass to steer you toward making choices that are true to who you are.
- Those who accept you for who you are and who support your authenticity should be in your sphere of influence. You may increase your self-confidence and feel more at ease expressing your true self by surrounding yourself with encouraging people.
- Question societal expectations by realizing that they may not always reflect your own best interests. Instead of simply following what is expected of you, analyse these assumptions, and make decisions that are consistent with your values and beliefs to challenge them.

- Recognize that no one is perfect and accept yourself for who you are by practicing self-acceptance and self-compassion. Be kind to yourself and cultivate self-compassion even when you falter or encounter difficulties.

- Self-reflection: Make time to regularly consider your thoughts, feelings, and actions. This can aid in increasing your self-awareness and enabling you to spot when you are performing dishonestly. Utilize this information to change your actions and beliefs to better fit with your genuine self.

- Get professional assistance: Seeing a therapist or counsellor for assistance can be beneficial if you are having trouble balancing your sense of self-authenticity with the demands of society. They can provide you the tools and techniques you need to go over these obstacles and develop a more genuine self.

**Fear of judgment and rejection**

Have you ever felt like you couldn't be your true self because of a fear of being judged or rejected? You're definitely not alone in feeling this way, as it's a common fear that many people experience.

Unfortunately, this fear can be detrimental to our self-authenticity. It can cause us to conform to societal standards or other people's opinions, rather than being true to ourselves. This can lead to a lack of self-awareness and self-esteem, which can ultimately impact our well-being and happiness.

Another challenge that comes with fear of criticism and rejection is difficulty in being assertive and setting boundaries. It can make us feel powerless and disempowered, which can impact our ability to express our true selves.

It's important to remember that embracing who you are is essential for personal growth and fulfillment. While it can be scary to show your true self, it's worth it in the end. Being true to yourself can lead to a more fulfilling and authentic life.

If you struggle with fear of judgment and rejection, know that there are ways to overcome these fears. Talking to a therapist or counsellor can provide you with support and tools to overcome these challenges. Remember, being true to yourself is a journey, but it's worth it in the end.

## What is the way forward?

Self-reflection, self-acceptance, and assertiveness training can be used to overcome the issue of how fear of criticism and rejection stifles self-authenticity.

## These are some helpful, realistic actions.

- Determine the origin of your anxiety by thinking about what makes you afraid of being rejected and judged in the first place. It might be a memory from the past, a conviction, or a way of thinking. Identifying the cause of your fear can help you create coping mechanisms.
- Practice self-acceptance: Being accepting of who you are can help you develop self-esteem and confidence. It may also make it simpler to express who you really are without worrying about criticism or rejection.
- Encourage positive self-talk: Talking badly to yourself can make you feel more anxious and insecure. Positive affirmations should be used to counter negative ideas.
- Develop your assertiveness: Being assertive implies defending your rights while respecting those of others. Training in assertiveness can assist you in expressing yourself in a courteous and confident manner without worrying about criticism or rejection.

- Create a network of support: Surround yourself with those who value your authenticity and accept you for who you are. Having someone to chat to while you're feeling weak or battling dread can be beneficial.

## Conditioning and Self Doubt

Years of conditioning may have left us doubting our own abilities and beliefs. We could not trust our own judgment since we're so accustomed to agreeing with what other people think. This may cause us to mistrust our own sincerity and self.

Self-authenticity can be hampered by conditioning and self-doubt because they might distort how we see ourselves and our actual aspirations, ideals, and beliefs.

The term "conditioning" describes the process of picking up on and conforming to our surroundings and societal standards. Positive and negative conditioning are both capable of subtly influencing our attitudes and actions.

For instance, if we were raised in a family or community that stressed obedience and conformity, we might experience pressure to uphold those ideals even if they don't reflect who we really are. This may cause us to repress our true desires, feelings, and ideas.

Moreover, self-doubt can hinder our capacity for authenticity. When we doubt ourselves, we could doubt our skills, wisdom, and deserving. This could cause us to look for approval from others or refrain from taking chances that might result in personal development and fulfilment.

Both training and self-doubt can create a gap between our genuine selves and the persona we show to the world. It can be exhausting and confusing to feel as though we are hiding behind a mask. It may also stop us from following our passions and leading a life that is consistent with our ideals.

It's critical to consider our training and ideas and to consider whether they reflect who we are as people in order to overcome these obstacles. In order to overcome self-doubt and increase our confidence in our abilities and worthiness, we can also practice self-compassion and self-acceptance.

In addition, getting assistance from dependable family, friends, or a mental health professional can be beneficial in overcoming these obstacles and promoting self-authenticity.

**Difficulty in letting go of masks and facades.**

Have you ever found it challenging to let go of the masks and facades you've put up in order to fit in or protect yourself? It's a common struggle that many people face when trying to embrace their true selves.

Unfortunately, this difficulty can severely impact our self-authenticity. When we're constantly hiding behind masks and facades, we're not able to express our true selves or live in accordance with our values and beliefs. Instead, we may present ourselves in a way that's not authentic just to fit in or avoid vulnerability.

The problem with this is that it can make it challenging for us to connect with others on a deeper level. When we're not being true to ourselves, our relationships can become shallow and unfulfilling, which can leave us feeling misunderstood and unloved. It can also make us feel lonely, anxious, and depressed because we're not being honest with ourselves or others.

In order to truly embrace authenticity, we need to be honest with ourselves and others about who we are, what we believe, and what we want. This requires bravery, openness, and self-awareness. It may also require seeking help from dependable friends, family, or mental health experts who can support us in overcoming any anxieties or insecurities holding us back.

But the benefits of embracing authenticity are worth it. It can lead to more fruitful and joyful lives, deeper and more meaningful connections, greater fulfillment in our personal and professional lives, and a sense of inner peace and contentment that comes from living in accordance with our values and beliefs. So, let's shed those masks and facades and embrace our true selves.

**The way forward**

If you're struggling to let go of masks and facades and embrace your true self, don't worry, it's a process that takes time and effort. But there are some steps you can take to move towards greater self-authenticity.

The first step is to recognize the masks and facades you've been wearing. Try to pinpoint the ways you present yourself differently depending on the circumstance and understand the motivations behind your choices. This will help you become more self-aware and take the next steps towards authenticity.

Next, try to comprehend why you put on masks and facades in the first place. Are you trying to blend in with a certain crowd or protect yourself from disapproval or criticism? Understanding the motivations behind your behaviour can help you address them and move towards greater authenticity.

It's also important to examine your assumptions and beliefs more closely. Challenge the beliefs that support your masks and facades and seek evidence that opposes them. This can help you develop a more accurate perception of yourself and your surroundings.

Being vulnerable can be uncomfortable, but it's an essential part of authenticity. Practice being more vulnerable by sharing your thoughts and feelings with dependable friends or family members. This can help you build the confidence you need to be more authentic in other areas of your life.

Finally, it's important to accept your individuality and realize the worth and value of being true to who you are. Honour the qualities that set you apart from others and celebrate your weaknesses.

Remember, if you're struggling to let go of masks and facades, consider seeking assistance from a therapist or counsellor. They can provide you with the tools and techniques you need to overcome your anxieties and take steps towards developing a more authentic self.

Embracing authenticity is a journey, but by following these steps, you can start leading a more genuine and satisfying life.

Here are some actions that can assist you in moving toward greater self-authenticity if you are having trouble letting go of masks and facades:

- Recognize your masks and facades: The first stage is to become aware of the masks and facades that you have been wearing. Try to pinpoint the ways you present yourself differently depending on the circumstance, as well as the motivations behind your choices.

- Know why you put on masks and facades: Try to comprehend the motivations behind your masks and facades after you have recognized them. Are you attempting to blend in with a certain crowd? Are you concerned about getting exposed? Are you attempting to defend yourself against disapproval or criticism?

- Examine your assumptions and beliefs more closely. Examine the assumptions and beliefs that support your masks and facades. Do they reflect reality or are they twisted by anxiety or fear? By seeking evidence that opposes them, one might challenge these convictions and presumptions.

- Practice being vulnerable: Being vulnerable can be uncomfortable at first, but it's a necessary part of authenticity. Work your build up to being more vulnerable and honest with others by beginning by sharing your ideas and feelings with dependable friends or family members.

- Accept your individuality: Realize the worth and value of being true to who you are. Honour your qualities that set you apart from others and celebrate your weaknesses.

- Get assistance: If you are having trouble letting go of masks and façades, think about getting assistance from a therapist or counsellor. They can provide you the tools and techniques you need to face your anxieties and take steps toward developing a truer self.

Just keep in mind that letting go of masks and façades is a lengthy process. But by following these instructions, you can begin to lead a more genuine and satisfying life.

## Lack of self-awareness

Have you ever found yourself behaving in a way that doesn't feel like the "real" you? It's a common experience, and it's often due to a lack of self-awareness. Self-awareness is crucial for understanding and expressing our true selves. It's the ability to reflect on our thoughts, feelings, and actions and relate them to our values, beliefs, and identities. When we lack self-awareness, we may not fully understand our motivations and desires, leading us to act in ways that don't align with our true selves.

This can lead to a sense of disconnection and unease, as we struggle to reconcile our actions with our beliefs. It can also make it difficult to communicate effectively with others, leading to misunderstandings and conflicts.

Fortunately, there are ways to cultivate self-awareness and increase our authenticity. By taking time for introspection and reflection, we can gain a better understanding of our values, strengths, and weaknesses. We can also pay attention to how our thoughts and behaviours align with our beliefs and make adjustments as needed.

Therapy and counselling can also be helpful in developing self-awareness, as they provide a safe and supportive space to explore our inner selves and gain new perspectives.

Ultimately, increasing our self-awareness is essential for living an authentic life. By understanding who we are and what we stand for, we can make choices that align with our values and lead to greater fulfillment and happiness.

**How to resolve the issue.**

Seek out new experiences and challenges that may help you gain a better understanding of yourself. This could include trying new hobbies or activities, traveling to new places, or meeting new people. • Reflect on past experiences and how they have shaped you. This can help you gain insight into your values and beliefs, and how they influence your decisions and behaviour. • Take personality or self-assessment tests to gain a deeper understanding of your strengths, weaknesses, and tendencies. • Practice self-compassion and self-forgiveness. Recognize that self-awareness is a lifelong process and that it's okay to make mistakes and learn from them. • Set aside time each day for introspection and reflection. This can include meditation, journaling, or simply taking a few moments to check in with yourself and your feelings. By taking these actions, you can begin to cultivate greater self-awareness and move toward a more authentic and fulfilling life.

## Low self-esteem

It's important to address low self-esteem in order to overcome the obstacles it presents to self-authenticity. Here are some steps you can take to build your self-esteem and become more authentic:

• Practice self-compassion: Treat yourself with kindness and understanding, just as you would treat a close friend. Be mindful of your self-talk and avoid negative self-judgments.

• Challenge negative beliefs: Identify negative beliefs about yourself that are holding you back and challenge them. Ask yourself if they are true, and if not, replace them with positive affirmations.

• Set realistic goals: Start with small, achievable goals and work your way up to bigger ones. Accomplishing these goals can help build your confidence and self-esteem.

• Focus on your strengths: Identify your strengths and accomplishments and celebrate them. Use them as a source of confidence and motivation.

• Surround yourself with positivity: Surround yourself with people who are supportive and positive. Avoid people who bring you down or make you feel bad about yourself.

• Seek professional help: Consider talking to a therapist or counsellor who can provide support and guidance in building your self-esteem and becoming more authentic.

Remember, building self-esteem takes time and effort, but the rewards of living a more authentic and fulfilling life are worth it.

If you have low self-esteem, you may find it difficult to be authentic because you are preoccupied with worrying about what others will think of you.

Since low self-esteem can make it difficult for you to convey your genuine thoughts, feelings, and values, it can be extremely difficult for you to be authentic. Low self-esteem might cause you to repress your true self and live up to others' expectations because they believe your thoughts are unworthy or unimportant.

For instance, if you are person with poor self-esteem you could refrain from advocating for oneself or expressing your wants or preferences out of concern that others will be reject or judge you. Also, you might find it difficult to set up strong boundaries or stand up for your morals, preferring to agree with others' viewpoints in order to blend in or be accepted.

Low self-esteem can also cause you to question your skills and potential, causing you to avoid opportunities or challenges that might allow you to completely express your true self. Have you ever practiced self-destructive habits or unfavourable self-talk, which further undermine your feeling of authenticity and self-worth?

In general, low self-esteem might prevent you from being truly authentic since it prevents you from expressing yourself fully and pursuing your dreams. Additionally, practicing self-care can also be helpful in addressing low self-esteem and promoting self-authenticity. This can include engaging in activities that bring joy and fulfillment, taking care of physical health through exercise and healthy eating, and setting aside time for relaxation and stress reduction.

It's important to remember that addressing low self-esteem and promoting self-authenticity is a process and may require ongoing effort and practice. However, by taking proactive steps and seeking support when needed, individuals can develop a stronger sense of self and live a more fulfilling and authentic life.

## Unresolved issues

By following these steps, people can address unresolved issues and work towards living a more authentic life. It's important to remember that resolving these issues can be a challenging and emotional process, but the end result of living in alignment with one's true self is worth the effort.

Unresolved issues can prevent us from living authentically. Unresolved issues can provide considerable hurdles to self-authenticity, which is the ability to recognize and express one's genuine self in thoughts, feelings, and actions. Unresolved Issues may have the following effects on self-authenticity:

• Unresolved concerns can cause emotional inhibition, in which people hide their genuine emotions and ideas in order to avoid facing their troubles. Lack of self-awareness and an inability to express oneself honestly can come from this.

• Lack of Clarity: Unresolved conflicts can cloud our thoughts and feelings, making it difficult to know who we are and what we want. It might be challenging to express oneself truthfully when there is a lack of clarity.

• Unresolved problems can cause self-doubt and a lack of trust in a person's skills and judgment. As a result, it may be difficult for people to express themselves honestly because they may doubt or question their genuine sentiments and thoughts.

• Creating Genuine Connections Can Be Difficult: Genuine relationships are based on respect, understanding, and trust. Building these kinds of relationships can be difficult for people who have unresolved difficulties, since they may find it difficult to be open and vulnerable with others.

• Setting Boundaries Can Be Difficult: People may find it difficult to understand and express their needs and limitations as a result of unresolved issues. This can make setting boundaries difficult. Because of this, building and maintaining genuine relationships with other people might be difficult. In conclusion, unaddressed conflicts can seriously undermine self-authenticity in a variety of ways. For people to comprehend and express their genuine selves authentically, they must address and resolve these challenges. How to resolve the issue? Unresolved problems can be difficult to resolve, however the following steps can be helpful:

• Identify the Problems: Identifying the problems is the first step in tackling unresolved problems. To identify the underlying reasons of the issue, some introspection and self-reflection may be necessary. In this process, journaling and talking to a therapist or trusted friend might be beneficial.

• Accept Responsibility: It's crucial to accept responsibility for the problems once you've discovered them. This entails admitting your part in causing or sustaining the issue and being prepared to contribute to finding a solution.

• Get Assistance: Seeing a licensed therapist or counsellor for assistance may be required, depending on the seriousness and complexity of the problems. A therapist can assist you in exploring your feelings and emotions, spotting behavioural patterns, and coming up with solutions to the problems.

• Exercise Self-Compassion: It can be a challenging and emotional process to deal with unsolved concerns, so it's crucial to practice self-compassion as you go. This entails treating oneself with compassion and understanding, acknowledging your successes and failures, and allowing yourself the necessary time and space for healing.

• Take Action: Last but not least, addressing unresolved situations requires taking action. This could entail altering your conduct, establishing limits, expressing regret to other people, or requesting forgiveness. As these actions may take some time and effort to complete, it is crucial to remain persistent and patient.

## Fear of Vulnerability

The fear of vulnerability is a common concern that individuals may have about revealing their genuine thoughts, emotions, and experiences. Vulnerability refers to the willingness to expose oneself to the possibility of emotional pain or rejection, and for some people, the fear of vulnerability can be a significant obstacle to expressing their authentic self.

When we fear vulnerability, we may hesitate to share our true feelings or ideas with others because we fear being judged or rejected. This can lead to a lack of authenticity in our relationships with others, as well as within ourselves. We may begin to hold back from expressing our true selves, and instead, present a version of ourselves that we believe will be more acceptable or less vulnerable.

The fear of vulnerability can also affect our ability to build meaningful and lasting relationships with others. When we are afraid to be vulnerable, we may struggle to form deep connections with others or to trust others with our innermost thoughts and feelings. This can result in relationships that feel shallow or unfulfilling, which can further erode our sense of self-authenticity.

In order to overcome the fear of vulnerability and live a more authentic life, it is important to recognize and challenge our fears, take calculated risks, and accept that vulnerability is a necessary component of personal growth and connection with others. By embracing vulnerability, we can build deeper and more meaningful relationships, and live a more fulfilling and authentic life.

### How to overcome the fear of vulnerability

Here are some strategies that can help you overcome the fear of vulnerability and embrace authenticity:

• Recognize the benefits of vulnerability: Being vulnerable can be a source of strength and connection, as it allows us to be honest about our experiences and emotions, which can help us build deeper and more meaningful relationships with others.

• Practice self-compassion: Practice treating yourself with kindness and understanding, rather than self-judgment and criticism. Self-compassion can help you develop a more positive self-image, which can make it easier to be vulnerable with others.

• Start small: Begin by expressing your thoughts and feelings in a low risk setting, such as with a trusted friend or family member. This can help you build confidence and gradually expand your comfort zone.

• Challenge your negative self-talk: Recognize and challenge any negative beliefs you may have about vulnerability and replace them with positive and realistic beliefs.

• Embrace imperfection: Accept that vulnerability involves the risk of rejection or failure, and that it is a natural part of the human experience. Embracing imperfection can help you overcome the fear of vulnerability and embrace authenticity.

• Get support: Seek the support of a therapist or counsellor, who can help you identify and address the underlying causes of your fear of vulnerability and provide you with tools and techniques to overcome it. Overcoming the fear of vulnerability is a gradual process, but with persistence and patience, it is possible to embrace authenticity and experience more fulfilling and meaningful relationships with others.

# Chapter Three

## AUTHENTICITY AND CONFORMITY

Conformity involves following societal norms and expectations, even if they conflict with one's own beliefs or values. Conformity can be motivated by a desire for acceptance or fear of rejection, as well as a belief that following the crowd is the "right" thing to do. While conformity may provide a sense of belonging and security, it can also result in a lack of individuality and a disconnection from one's true self. When we conform instead of being authentic, we may feel like we are wearing a mask or playing a role rather than living as our genuine selves. This can lead to feelings of dissatisfaction, lack of fulfilment, and even depression. In contrast, when we live authentically, we experience a sense of congruence between our inner selves and outer expressions, leading to a sense of fulfilment and contentment. In conclusion, self-authenticity and conformity represent two different ways of living and making decisions. While conformity may offer temporary benefits such as acceptance and security, it ultimately prevents us from fully expressing our true selves and can lead to a sense of disconnection and dissatisfaction. Being authentic, on the other hand, allows us to live a life that is true to our values and beliefs, leading to a greater sense of fulfilment and purpose.

## What Is Conformity

conformity involves altering our behaviour to fit in with a broader group or culture, which may require sacrificing our self-authenticity. While it can be a useful tool for socialization, it can also lead us to adopt values and beliefs that don't align with our own. Being mindful of when to conform and when to stand up for our authentic selves can help us live a life true to our own values and beliefs.

Both self-authenticity and conformity have their benefits and drawbacks. It's important to strike a balance between them and to choose the approach that aligns with our values and beliefs while also respecting others and the society we live in. Being authentic can be challenging, but it can also lead to a more fulfilling and satisfying life. Conforming can be comfortable, but it can also lead to a lack of personal growth and critical thinking. Ultimately, the key is to be mindful and intentional in our choices and actions.

## Overcoming Conformity Pressure

You are familiar with the pressure of conformity—the sensation that you must say or do something for others to accept or like you. In such a setting, it may be challenging to stand out from the throng and be unique.

Here are some strategies for overcoming the demands of conformity if you wish to embrace self-authenticity:

• Practice Mindfulness. Mindfulness entails being present in the moment and fully aware of your thoughts and feelings. By practicing mindfulness, you can tune out external distractions and concentrate on your internal compass. This can help you stay true to yourself and prevent you from being swayed by the opinions of others.

• Be Prepared to Disagree In order to be authentic, you must be willing to express your thoughts and opinions, even if they are different from those of others. Prepare yourself for disagreements or potential conflict by practicing active listening and being respectful of other people's perspectives, while still standing firm in your own beliefs.

• Don't Be Afraid to Say No One of the simplest ways to maintain your authenticity is to learn how to say "no" when you don't agree with something or don't want to do something. Saying "no" can be difficult, particularly in group settings, but it is crucial in order to honour your own values and priorities. By putting these strategies into practice, you can learn to overcome the pressure of conformity and embrace your true self. Remember that being authentic is a continuous process and requires courage, self-awareness, and a willingness to challenge the status quo.

# Chapter Four

## IDENTIFYING YOUR OWN VALUES AND BELIEFS

**What Do Your Individual Values and Beliefs Entail?**

Identifying your own values and beliefs is crucial to achieving self-authenticity because it allows you to live a life that is true to yourself. When you understand your values and beliefs, you can make choices that align with them and that are consistent with your true identity. This can help you to feel more fulfilled and satisfied with your life, as you are living in a way that is true to your own principles and convictions.

In addition, identifying your values and beliefs can help you to establish personal boundaries and make decisions that are in line with your own interests and goals. It can also help you to communicate more effectively with others, as you will have a clearer understanding of your own perspective and how it aligns (or doesn't align) with others.

Overall, identifying your values and beliefs is an essential part of developing self-authenticity, as it enables you to live a life that is true to yourself and that aligns with your own sense of purpose and meaning.

**What Your Core Values Are.**

To identify your core values, you can also consider the following questions:

1. What makes you happy?
2. What motivates and inspires you?
3. What are you most passionate about?
4. What are your top priorities in life?
5. What are your non-negotiables in relationships or friendships?
6. What makes you feel fulfilled?
7. What are your strengths and how do they inform your values?
8. What do you stand for?
9. What do you want to be remembered for?
10. What are some of the most important lessons you have learned in life?

By reflecting on these questions and taking the time to think about your responses, you can gain a deeper understanding of your core values and how they shape your life. Remember, it's okay for your values to change over time as you grow and learn more about yourself and the world around you.

**Developing Your Values.**

Developing your values is a continuous process that often involves making a lot of mistakes. You can use the following methods to identify the values that are most significant to you:

1. Self-reflection: Take some time to reflect on your life experiences and think about the values that were most important to you during those times. Ask yourself what beliefs or principles guided your decisions and actions.
2. Seeking feedback: Talk to people close to you and ask them to describe what they think are your core values. This can give you an outside perspective on what you hold dear and help you understand how others perceive you.
3. Reading and learning: Read books or articles on values and ethics to gain a deeper understanding of what values are and how they can influence your life. You can also attend workshops or seminars on values and ethics to learn from experts in the field.
4. Trying new things: Trying new experiences and challenges can help you discover new values or reinforce existing ones. Engage in activities that interest you or take on challenges that push you out of your comfort zone.
5. Making mistakes: Don't be afraid to make mistakes along the way. Making mistakes can be a valuable learning experience and can help you clarify your values and beliefs.

Remember, developing your values is a personal and ongoing process. Don't feel pressured to have everything figured out at once and be open to revising and refining your values as you grow and evolve.

**Reflect**

There are many milestones in life that can be significant and help shape our values and beliefs. Here are a few examples:

1.  Childhood: Our upbringing and experiences in childhood can shape our values and beliefs in significant ways. Family values, cultural traditions, and religious beliefs are often established during childhood.
2.  Adolescence: During adolescence, we begin to form our own identity and may question the values and beliefs we were taught as children. This is a time when we may experiment with new ideas and explore different ways of thinking.
3.  Education: Our experiences in school and the knowledge we gain can shape our values and beliefs. Education can expose us to different perspectives and help us develop critical thinking skills.
4.  Career: Our work can be a significant part of our lives and can shape our values and beliefs. We may prioritize financial success, work-life balance, or making a difference in the world.
5.  Relationships: Our relationships with family, friends, and romantic partners can also shape our values and beliefs. We may prioritize loyalty, honesty, or compassion in our relationships.
6.  Parenthood: Becoming a parent can be a significant milestone that shapes our values and beliefs. We may prioritize family, responsibility, and sacrifice.

It's important to reflect on the values and beliefs that are most important to us throughout these milestones and hold onto them as we move forward in life. By doing so, we can live a more authentic and fulfilling life.

**Look at your beliefs.**

Additionally, it's important to reflect on where these beliefs originated from. Were they influenced by your family, culture, or personal experiences? Examining the roots of your beliefs can help you better understand why they are important to you and how they shape your worldview.

It's also important to consider whether these beliefs are still relevant and meaningful to you. As we grow and evolve, our beliefs and values can shift and change. Reflecting on whether certain beliefs still align with your current values can help you ensure that you are living authentically and in line with your true self.

**Take some time to think.**

Spend some time reflecting and determining what is most important to you. Make a record of what happens throughout this period because it can help you understand some issues you hadn't previously considered.

Everyone seeking personal development and self-discovery should start by identifying their values and beliefs. It will be simpler for you to determine how to best align with those values in all facets of life if you take the time to reflect, consider your prior experiences and views, and get clear on what's vital.

Knowing your values and beliefs is essential for personal growth and development, as it allows you to align your actions and decisions with your true self. It's important to take the time to reflect and think about what is important to you, and to continually reassess and revise your values as you grow and change over time. This can lead to a more authentic and fulfilling life. I for living honestly.

**Examining Your Personal Values.**

Examining your personal values can help you prioritize your time and energy, allowing you to focus on what truly matters to you. This can lead to a sense of purpose and fulfillment in life. It can also help you make difficult decisions when faced with conflicting options by allowing you to evaluate which choice aligns with your values and beliefs.

It's important to note that personal values can change over time as we gain new experiences and perspectives. Regularly re-evaluating and reflecting on our values can help us stay aligned with our true selves and lead a more authentic life.

A solid and fulfilling existence depends on being genuine to oneself. Finding out what matters to you and what is essential to you might help you develop a feeling of self-authenticity.

Being honest with yourself about life, including your deepest wishes, goals, and any lingering concerns or uncertainties, is frequently the first step towards achieving this. Also, you can learn how to prioritize what matters in life by understanding your personal values and what makes you tick.

While investigating your values, it's crucial to:

- Give yourself some time to think about the important things.
- Pose challenging questions to yourself, such as "How do I want to spend my time?" What sort of partnerships am I looking for?

- Use this information to your decisions to help you stay true to who you are and what's important in life.

- Check that your behaviour is consistent with your beliefs and values.

Understanding your values can help you become clearer about the life you want for yourself, which is essential for developing self-authenticity. Making decisions that reflect those beliefs then becomes simpler since all that is left to do is ask yourself, "Is this decision in accordance with who I truly am?"

## A Look at Your Beliefs

Have you ever given your values and beliefs serious consideration? Although it's not always simple to identify them, knowing your values and beliefs is crucial to living a life that is authentic to who you are.

Understanding your beliefs is crucial since they form the foundation of who we are. Before you begin your research, consider the following queries:

- What is most important to me?

- How do I fit into the world?

- How do my actions conflict with my principles?

- What would I sacrifice for a cause I support?

- How can I use my convictions to change the world?

Your values are the precepts and concepts that direct your behaviour; they originate from within and influence how you set priorities, deal with people, and make choices. Asking yourself this will help you better understand your values:

1. What objectives will enable me to meet my own standards?

2. What character traits ought I to aspire to?

3. Are there any circumstances in which I have trouble making decisions? Then why?

4. How do I view achievement and failure?

You can learn more about who you are and what important to you by thoughtfully answering these questions. Creating a life that truly reflects your values and beliefs requires you to take this action.

## How to Make Choices With This Information

By understanding your personal values and beliefs and using them as a guide for your decisions and actions, you can live a more authentic and fulfilling life. It may take time and effort to develop this self-awareness, but the benefits are well worth it. Regular reflection on your values and beliefs can help you stay true to yourself and make choices that align with your priorities. It can also help you navigate difficult situations where you may face pressure to conform or compromise your values. Remember, being authentic doesn't mean being perfect, but rather being true to yourself and your principles. Taking a personal perspective on each choice is the first step. Based on your principles and beliefs, are you making this decision? Why not, if not? It is crucial to take the time to evaluate each choice considering your own standards since doing so will enable you to make better educated choices that are true to your character.

Also, it's critical to be conscious of the ways in which others close to you affect your choices. Checking in with oneself on a frequent basis is important since it's simple to lose sight of our own principles and beliefs when we're around people who might hold different opinions.

Finally, let conversations with people be influenced by your understanding of your views and values. Knowing what matters most to you will offer you a solid foundation for any conversation, whether it be debating politics with friends or working decisions with co-workers.

## Personal values and beliefs reflection

Self-reflection has a crucial role in determining your personal values and ideas. It can be a beneficial mental and spiritual activity to take the time to reflect carefully on your values and the reasons behind them.

It could be beneficial to reflect on yourself by asking yourself the following questions:

- What life events have been the most significant to me?
- What, in my opinion, constitutes a successful life?
- How do I react when circumstances arise that go against my morals or beliefs?
- What kind of personal commitments am I ready to accept?
- When I reflect on my life, what lessons have I taken away?

Being conscious of your thoughts, feelings, and reactions can help you gain a deeper understanding of your values as well as reveal any previously unknown hidden beliefs. You can find patterns in your behaviour and learn more about yourself by asking yourself the questions mentioned above (or any other questions that come to mind organically).

In addition to asking these questions, it can also be helpful to keep a journal or a log of your thoughts and reflections. Writing down your responses to these questions, as well as any other insights you gain through self-reflection, can help you see patterns and themes in your beliefs and values over time. This can also serve as a useful reference point when faced with difficult decisions or when trying to stay true to your values in challenging situations.

Remember, the process of identifying and understanding your personal values and beliefs is ongoing and evolving. As you grow and change, your values and beliefs may also shift and develop. Embrace the journey of self-discovery and continue to reflect on your values and beliefs as you navigate life's challenges and opportunities.

# Chapter Five

---

## SELF AUTHENTICATION AND SELF DISCOVERY

Every person embarks on a path of self-discovery at some point in their life. It is a process of self-exploration and self-understanding that entails learning about one's traits, flaws, beliefs, values, and purpose. Self-discovery is an essential process that helps people find their genuine selves, which in turn helps them live authentically fulfilled lives. Self-authenticity is a crucial component of self-discovery because it enables people to recognize their genuine selves and lead lives that are consistent with their moral principles and worldviews. Self-discovery is not always a straightforward process. It necessitates that people face their worries, uncertainties, and concerns. Nonetheless, because it enables people to lead true, fulfilled lives, the process of self-discovery is worth the effort. Here are a few essential ideas that illustrate how self-discovery and self-authenticity are related.

1. Self-discovery involves exploring and understanding one's own beliefs, values, and purpose. This process helps individuals gain a deeper understanding of their true selves and allows them to live in accordance with their own unique principles and worldview.

2. Self-authenticity is the practice of living a life that is true to one's own values and beliefs. It involves being honest with oneself and living in a way that aligns with one's true identity.

3. Self-discovery and self-authenticity go hand in hand. The process of self-discovery is necessary for individuals to identify their genuine selves and determine what is important to them. Self-authenticity is the natural outcome of this process as individuals begin to live in accordance with their true selves.

4. Self-discovery and self-authenticity enable individuals to live fulfilling lives. By knowing oneself and living authentically, individuals can make choices that are consistent with their values and beliefs, leading to a greater sense of purpose and satisfaction.

5. The journey of self-discovery and self-authenticity is ongoing. It requires constant self-reflection and evaluation as individuals grow and change throughout their lives. By remaining open and willing to learn more about oneself, individuals can continue to live authentically and lead fulfilling lives.

**Self-Awareness Comes from Self-Discovery.**

Self-discovery requires self-awareness as a crucial element. Understanding one's thoughts, feelings, and behaviours is a necessary component of self-awareness. It allows people to understand their strengths and limitations and pinpoint areas where they can grow personally.

People experience a greater sense of self-awareness as they set out on a journey of self-discovery. They start to recognize their distinctive personality features, beliefs, values, and objectives. People develop a deeper grasp of their true selves through self-reflection and introspection.

## Self-Discovery makes self-acceptance possible.

A key component of self-authenticity is self-acceptance. People are more likely to express themselves honestly and without pretence when they embrace themselves for who they are. Self-acceptance entails accepting oneself completely, regardless of one's flaws or qualities.

More self-awareness, which comes from self-discovery, enables people to accept themselves for who they are. People can pinpoint the qualities they enjoy in themselves as well as the areas they would like to improve through self-reflection and introspection. The ability to live an authentic and true to oneself life is made possible by this process of self-acceptance.

## Self-Discovery Makes Self-Expression Possible.

A key element of self-authenticity is self-expression. People are more likely to feel fulfilled and satisfied with their lives when they express themselves honestly and without pretence. Self-expression entails being authentic in how one expresses to others their thoughts, feelings, and ideas.

Self-expression requires a keen sense of self-acceptance. When individuals embrace themselves for who they are, they are more likely to express themselves truly. They are less inclined to conceal who they really are or act else.

## Self-Discovery Allows for Self-Fulfilment

The goal of self-authenticity is self-fulfilment. People are more likely to feel content and satisfied with their lives when they lead authentic lifestyles. Achieving one's objectives, leading a moral life, and being authentic in one's expression are all components of self-fulfilment.

Self-fulfilment depends heavily on self-expression. Genuine communication increases a person's chances of success and helps them live a life that is consistent with their ideals. They are more likely to experience life satisfaction and fulfilment.

## Self-Discovery Promotes Personal Development

Self-discovery is critically dependent on personal progress. Those who set out on a journey of self-discovery are likely to run into difficulties and roadblocks. Nonetheless, these difficulties offer chances for development and improvement on a personal level.

Introspection and self-reflection allow people to discover their own areas of personal development.

## Understanding One's Limiting Beliefs Helps in Self-Discovery

Limiting beliefs are unfavourable attitudes and thoughts that prevent people from realizing their greatest potential. They can be strongly imprinted and are frequently created early in life. People are less likely to be restricted by limiting views and more likely to succeed when they are genuine to themselves.

### Self-Discovery Helps in the Development of Self-Compassion

The capacity to be understanding and compassionate to oneself is known as self-compassion. It means treating oneself with the same care and consideration that one would offer to a close friend. To develop self-compassion, people need to be able to see themselves clearly and recognize their strengths and weaknesses. This can be done through self-discovery. People are more likely to be genuine to themselves and lead real lives when they are kind and empathetic to themselves.

### Self-Discovery Helps in Developing Resilience

Being resilient means having the capacity to overcome challenges. It is a crucial quality that can aid people in coping with life's ups and downs. By enabling people to recognize their strengths and shortcomings and to develop coping mechanisms for dealing with difficulties, self-discovery can aid people in developing resilience. People are more likely to be resilient and overcome adversity when they are genuine to themselves.

### Self-Discovery Promotes the Development of Genuine Partnerships

Honesty, openness, and respect are the pillars of an authentic partnership. Being truthful to oneself increases the likelihood of attracting and sustaining genuine connections. Those who are self-aware can better define their ideals and link themselves with like-minded people. People are more likely to feel encouraged and lead authentic lives when they are surrounded by authentic relationships.

### Self-Ddiscovery promotes Self-Esteem.

Self-esteem is the degree to which individuals appreciate themselves. It is crucial for maintaining mental health and wellbeing. By enabling people to recognize their strengths and appreciate their achievements, self-discovery can help people feel better about themselves. People are more likely to be true to themselves and lead real, fulfilling lives when they have a high sense of self-worth.

## Self-Discovery Aids in Confidence Building

Confidence is the conviction that one can succeed. It is a crucial quality that can aid people in reaching their objectives. Self-discovery enables people to recognize their talents and create plans for overcoming their deficiencies, which can help them gain confidence. Those who exude confidence are more inclined to be honest with themselves and pursue their goals with zeal and excitement.

## Tools for Self-Discovery

Although being authentic is not simple, there are several techniques you may do to help you become truer to yourself. First and foremost, it's critical to have the ability to stay true to oneself without abandoning others.

Here are some suggestions for tools:

## Listen to your true emotions!

Checking in with your emotions is the best approach to get started on the path of honesty. Being honest about your feelings, both positive and negative, includes asking yourself how you genuinely feel at any particular time. Even though it's frequently simpler stated than done, cultivating authenticity can be greatly aided by knowing how to recognize and communicate your actual emotions.

### Exercise courage

The ability to be vulnerable and defend your beliefs in the face of criticism or disapproval from others is a quality that authenticity demands. Making errors can be frightening, but it's the only way to develop and discover our true selves. Instead of fearing failure, develop courage!

### Make up a Real-Life Narrative

Our feeling of self-authenticity is significantly influenced by our personal tales. Spend some time thinking about the things that have shaped your life to date—the people, places, and experiences that have shaped who you are today—in order to write a more real story. Check your story to see if there are any gaps or inconsistencies that need be filled in or adjustments that should be made so that it more accurately reflects who you are and who you aspire to be moving forward.

### The Influence of Being Yourself

Being genuine to oneself has tremendous power. Being self-authentic is feeling at ease in your own skin and being wholly genuine. The only thing that matters is how you feel; what other people think is irrelevant.

This is crucial to leading a successful life since it increases our sense of satisfaction and fulfilment in our endeavours. Being true to oneself has various advantages, including the following:

### Locate Your Voice

By embracing our unique voice, we not only honour our individuality but also contribute to the diversity of perspectives in the world. Our distinct experiences, narratives, and viewpoints are what make us human, and by sharing them, we can inspire, educate, and empower others.

However, it's not always easy to be true to ourselves, especially when we feel pressure to conform to social norms or expectations. It can be tempting to wear masks and hide our true selves, but doing so only leads to feelings of disconnection and dissatisfaction.

To live an authentic life, we must be willing to take off the masks and speak our truth. We must be willing to embrace ourselves completely, with all our flaws and imperfections, and accept ourselves as we are.

It's a journey of self-discovery that requires courage, vulnerability, and self-compassion. But the rewards of living authentically are immeasurable. When we own our voice and speak our truth, we connect with others on a deeper level, build stronger relationships, and live a more fulfilling life.

So, let's embrace our unique voice, remove our masks, and express ourselves freely. Let's own who we are and share our authentic selves with the world. Because in doing so, we not only enrich our own lives but also inspire others to do the same.

## How to Preserve Your Self-Authenticity

One of the most effective strategies for living an authentic life is to be who you truly are. Here are some helpful pointers for becoming your most genuine self:

Following your intuition is a key aspect of being true to yourself. Your intuition, also known as your inner voice or gut feeling, is the voice that speaks to you from within. It can guide you towards what is right for you and help you make decisions that align with your values and beliefs.

It's important to recognize and respect your intuition, even if it goes against the opinions of others or society's expectations. By doing so, you can learn to trust yourself and your instincts, which can lead to greater confidence and self-assurance.

2.  Be Honest with Yourself: It's crucial to be honest with yourself about who you are, what you want, and what you believe in. This entails being true to your values and beliefs, as well as acknowledging your strengths and weaknesses.

Being honest with yourself also means recognizing when you may be living inauthentically, such as when you're trying to conform to the expectations of others or when you're not pursuing your true passions and interests. By acknowledging these areas of inauthenticity, you can work towards living a more authentic life.

3.  Express Yourself: Expressing yourself is a powerful way to live authentically. This can take many forms, such as through creative outlets like art, music, or writing, or through expressing your thoughts and feelings to others.

When you express yourself, you're sharing a part of yourself with the world and allowing others to see the real you. It can also help you connect with others who share similar interests and values, which can provide a sense of community and belonging.

4.  Embrace Your Imperfections: No one is perfect, and it's important to embrace your imperfections and flaws as a part of who you are. Accepting your imperfections can help you feel more comfortable in your own skin and prevent you from striving for an unattainable ideal.

Remember that your imperfections can also be your strengths, as they provide unique perspectives and experiences that can enrich your life and the lives of those around you.

5.  Set Boundaries: Setting boundaries is an important part of being true to yourself. This means establishing limits for yourself and others in order to protect your values, beliefs, and well-being.

Setting boundaries can involve saying no to activities or situations that don't align with your values or goals, or establishing boundaries with others who may be trying to influence or control you. By setting clear boundaries, you can protect your authenticity and ensure that you're living a life that is true to yourself.

Being true to yourself is a journey that requires self-awareness, honesty, and self-expression. By following these tips, you can become your most genuine self and live a more authentic and fulfilling life.

**Techniques for gaining self-awareness.**

The capacity to comprehend and recognize one's own feelings, ideas, and behaviours is known as self-awareness. It is an essential quality that aids in personality development, informed decision-making, and successful interpersonal connections.

Emotional intelligence, which is important in both personal and professional contexts, is fundamentally based on self-awareness. The basis for personal development and growth is self-awareness. Being aware of one's emotions, values, beliefs, strengths, and shortcomings is a requirement.

Introspection, reflection, and self-evaluation are all parts of the ongoing process of developing self-awareness. Self-aware persons are more likely to comprehend their emotions and how they affect their actions, thoughts, and behaviours. Also, they are better at controlling their emotions and responding appropriately to various situations.

Self-awareness has many advantages, including better decision-making, enhanced interpersonal interactions, and enhanced communication skills. Due to the fact that they are aware of their own communication style and how it may affect others, self-conscious people are better communicators.

Since they are able to evaluate their own prejudices and identify when they are being influenced by outside influences, they are also more adept at making decisions. Also, because they are aware of their needs and are able to express them clearly to others, self-conscious people are more likely to establish and sustain successful relationships.

So how do we raise our level of self-awareness? Self-reflection exercise is the first stage. This entails reflecting on your feelings, thoughts, and actions as they pertain to various situations. It's critical to be honest with yourself and recognize your advantages and disadvantages. Maintaining a journal to record your thoughts and emotions could also be beneficial.

Seeking out other people's opinions is another method for enhancing self-awareness. This can be difficult because it calls for tolerance for criticism, but it can also be a useful tool for personal development. Critique can be provided by close friends, relatives, co-workers, or even a therapist. It is crucial to pay close attention to the input and consider how your own self-perception is affected by it.

Finally, mindfulness exercises like yoga or meditation can enhance self-awareness. Being mindful means paying attention and observing your thoughts and feelings without passing judgment. You can use it to spot trends in your emotions and behaviour and pinpoint potential areas for improvement.

In summary, self-awareness is an essential quality for success in both personal and professional endeavours. It entails comprehending and identifying your feelings, ideas, and behaviours as well as how they relate to various circumstances.

Those who are self-aware are better at communicating, making decisions, and maintaining healthy relationships. It is crucial to engage in self-reflection, solicit feedback, and engage in mindfulness exercises to increase self-awareness. Anybody can increase their self-awareness and benefit from it with persistent practice and effort.

## Identifying Limiting Beliefs and Self-Imposed Restrictions

Self-imposed limitations and limiting beliefs will certainly prevent us from attaining our goals and leading satisfying lives. These thoughts are frequently strongly embedded in our mind, making it challenging to identify and get rid of them. But, with some self-reflection and mindfulness, it is feasible to identify and break free from these restraints.

## What do limiting beliefs entail?

Our potential is restricted by limiting assumptions we have about ourselves, other people, or the world at large. These ideas, which may or may not be conscious, are frequently based on previous encounters, conditioning, and cultural or societal conventions.

Typical limiting beliefs include:

- "I'm not up to it."
- "I'm not deserving of achievement."
- "I'm too old/young."
- "Money is not for me."
- "I'm not talented enough.

These ideas may keep us from following our interests, taking chances, and accomplishing our objectives. They generate a negative mindset that encourages self-doubt and dread, leading to a cycle of self-sabotage.

**How to spot restricting thoughts.**

1. Notice your inner voice: Your inner voice is the dialogue that goes on inside your mind. Pay attention to what you are saying to yourself. If you hear yourself making negative comments, such as "I can't do it," or "I'm not good enough," then those are limiting beliefs.
2. Recognize patterns: Take a look at your past experiences and see if you can identify any recurring patterns. For example, if you always seem to give up when things get tough, then you may have a limiting belief that you are not capable of handling difficult situations.
3. Be aware of your reactions: Notice how you react to situations that challenge you. If you tend to feel anxious or avoidant in these situations, it could be a sign that you have limiting beliefs holding you back.
4. Pay attention to your language: The language you use can be a clue to your limiting beliefs. For example, if you often use words like "always" or "never," it could indicate a belief that you are stuck in a certain pattern and cannot change.
5. Seek feedback: Ask friends or family members for feedback on your behaviour or reactions. They may be able to identify patterns or beliefs that you are not aware of.

By identifying limiting beliefs, you can start to challenge them and develop a more positive mindset that will help you achieve your goals. It's important to be patient and compassionate with yourself throughout this process, as it can take time to change deeply ingrained beliefs.

**Pay attention to what your mind is saying!**

Once you've identified your limiting thoughts, it's important to challenge them. Ask yourself, "Is this thought really true?" or "Is there any evidence to support this belief?" Often, our limiting thoughts are based on assumptions or past experiences that may not be relevant to our current situation.

Examine the consequences of your beliefs! Another way to challenge your limiting thoughts is to consider the consequences of holding onto them. What impact do these beliefs have on your life? Are they helping or hindering your progress towards your goals? Sometimes, examining the consequences of our beliefs can help us realize that they are not serving us well.

Reframe your thoughts! Once you've challenged your limiting thoughts, try reframing them into more positive, empowering statements. For example, instead of "I'm not good enough to achieve my goals," reframe it as "I am capable of achieving my goals with hard work and dedication." Reframing our thoughts can help us overcome limiting beliefs and approach challenges with a more positive mindset.

Practice mindfulness! Practicing mindfulness can help us become more aware of our thoughts and feelings and notice when limiting beliefs arise. Mindfulness can also help us develop a more compassionate and accepting attitude towards ourselves, which can help us overcome our limiting beliefs with greater ease. By being aware of your inner dialogue and challenging your limiting beliefs, you can overcome them and live a more fulfilling and authentic life. Remember, your thoughts shape your reality, so it's important to make sure they are positive and empowering.

**Determine patterns.**

Limiting beliefs frequently show up as behavioural patterns. Search for thought and behaviour habits that might be preventing you from moving forward. For instance, it can be a symptom of a limiting belief if you routinely refrain from taking chances or pursuing your goals.

Consider alternative perspectives. Another effective method to identify limiting beliefs is to consider alternative perspectives. This entails stepping outside of your comfort zone and seeking out diverse viewpoints that challenge your own beliefs. For example, if you believe that you are not skilled enough to pursue a particular career path, seek out someone who has successfully pursued that path with a similar background or skillset.

Practice self-compassion. It is important to remember that limiting beliefs are often deeply ingrained and can take time and effort to overcome. Be kind to yourself and avoid self-judgment as you work through these beliefs. Practicing self-compassion can help you approach this process with a more open and positive mindset.

Seek support. Breaking through limiting beliefs can be a challenging and emotional process. Seek out support from trusted friends, family members, or professionals who can offer guidance and encouragement. It can also be helpful to join a support group or attend workshops or therapy sessions specifically focused on overcoming limiting beliefs. By using these techniques, you can begin to identify and challenge your limiting beliefs, allowing you to live a more fulfilling and authentic life. Remember that the process of identifying and overcoming limiting beliefs is ongoing and requires persistence and patience, but the rewards of living a more fulfilling life are well worth the effort.

**Receive criticism.**

It's important to note that limiting beliefs can come in various forms and impact every aspect of our lives. They can hold us back in our careers, relationships, personal growth, and overall well-being. Recognizing and challenging these beliefs is crucial to living an authentic and fulfilling life.

One common limiting belief is the idea that we are not good enough or worthy of success. This belief can manifest in different ways, such as avoiding challenges or opportunities that could lead to growth, settling for less than we deserve, or feeling imposter syndrome. To overcome this belief, we can practice self-compassion and acknowledge our strengths and achievements. It can also be helpful to reframe our thoughts and focus on the possibilities and opportunities rather than the limitations and failures.

Another limiting belief is the fear of failure or rejection. This belief can prevent us from taking risks or pursuing our passions and dreams. To challenge this belief, we can reframe failure as an opportunity for growth and learning rather than a sign of inadequacy. It can also be helpful to focus on the process rather than the outcome and celebrate our efforts and progress along the way.

## Overcoming Restrictive Assumptions

Redefine your self-talk. Once you have identified your limiting beliefs, it's time to reframe your self-talk to challenge and overcome them. Reframe the negative self-talk into positive affirmations and start repeating them to yourself regularly. This will help you to reinforce positive self-talk and weaken the hold of negative self-talk.

Seek evidence to the contrary. Look for evidence that contradicts your limiting beliefs. For example, if you believe you are not good enough to apply for a job, seek evidence of other people with similar experience and background who have successfully applied for and landed that job. This will help you to see that your beliefs are not necessarily true and give you more confidence to move forward.

Take small steps. Overcoming limiting beliefs can be daunting, so it's important to start with small steps. This will help you to build momentum and gain confidence as you move towards your goals. Celebrate your successes, no matter how small, and use them to motivate yourself to keep going.

Embrace failure. Failure is a natural part of growth and learning. Don't be afraid to try new things and fail. Use failure as a learning opportunity and an opportunity to grow. Embrace the discomfort and use it to push yourself forward.

Visualize success. Visualizing success is a powerful tool for overcoming limiting beliefs. Take time to visualize yourself succeeding in your goals and focus on the positive feelings associated with success. This will help to reinforce positive beliefs and weaken the hold of limiting beliefs.

Seek feedback. Getting feedback from others can be a helpful tool for overcoming limiting beliefs. Seek feedback from people you trust and ask them for honest and constructive feedback. Use this feedback to improve and grow, and to challenge any limiting beliefs you may have. By using these techniques, you can overcome your limiting beliefs and live a more fulfilling and authentic life. Remember that overcoming limiting beliefs is a process that takes time and effort, but the rewards are well worth it. With persistence and patience, you can break free from restrictive assumptions and live the life you truly desire.

**Change your perspective.**

Change your perspective. Change your perspective by substituting restrictive statements with empowering statements. As an illustration, if you think you're not good enough, tell yourself, "I am capable and deserving of success." This practice can help you build self-confidence and self-belief, which can eventually replace your limiting beliefs.

Gather evidence. It's critical to challenge your limiting beliefs with evidence to help you see things more objectively. Make a list of your accomplishments and strengths and use this list to challenge your limiting beliefs. For example, if you believe that you're not smart enough to start your own business, remind yourself of the times you've overcome challenges in the past or achieved success in a similar situation.

**Take action.**

Taking action is one of the most effective ways to overcome limiting beliefs. It's important to challenge yourself and take small steps towards your goals, even if you don't feel completely confident or ready. This can help you build momentum and self-assurance, which can in turn help you break through your limiting beliefs.

Seek support. Don't be afraid to seek out support from others as you work to overcome your limiting beliefs. Surround yourself with positive and supportive people who can encourage and motivate you. You may also want to consider seeking out a coach or therapist who can provide guidance and support as you work through your beliefs.

Practice self-compassion. As you work to overcome your limiting beliefs, it's important to practice self-compassion and be patient with yourself. Overcoming limiting beliefs can be a challenging process, and it's okay to make mistakes or encounter setbacks. Treat yourself with kindness and understanding and keep moving forward with determination and positivity.

By using these methods, you can begin to overcome your limiting beliefs and live a more fulfilling and authentic life. Remember, it's a process that requires patience and persistence, but the rewards of living a more confident and self-assured life are well worth the effort.

**Question your beliefs.**

Challenging your beliefs is an essential step in overcoming limiting assumptions. It involves questioning the validity of your beliefs and searching for evidence that contradicts them. One way to do this is to find examples of people who have overcome similar challenges and succeeded. This can help you see that your limiting belief may not be entirely accurate or applicable to your situation.

Another effective technique is to examine the evidence that supports your belief. Are there any logical fallacies or biases that may be affecting your thinking? Are there any alternate explanations that might be more accurate or realistic? Asking these types of questions can help you identify flaws in your thinking and open yourself up to new perspectives.

**Develop a growth mindset.**

A growth mindset is the belief that your abilities and intelligence can be developed through hard work and dedication. This is in contrast to a fixed mindset, which assumes that your abilities are fixed and unchangeable. By developing a growth mindset, you can overcome limiting beliefs by recognizing that your potential is not predetermined and that you can always improve and grow.

To develop a growth mindset, focus on the process of learning and growth rather than just the outcome. Embrace challenges as opportunities to learn and develop and view failure as a natural part of the learning process. By doing so, you can shift your focus from a fixed mindset to a growth mindset and open yourself up to new possibilities and opportunities.

**Take action.**

One of the most effective ways to overcome limiting beliefs is to take action. Often, limiting beliefs can prevent us from even attempting to pursue our goals and aspirations. By taking action, we can prove to ourselves that our limiting beliefs are not entirely accurate and that we are capable of achieving more than we thought.

Start by setting small goals and taking steps towards achieving them. Celebrate your successes along the way, no matter how small they may seem. By doing so, you can build momentum and confidence, and overcome your limiting beliefs one step at a time.

Seek support. Overcoming limiting beliefs can be a difficult and emotional process. Seek support from trusted friends, family members, or professionals who can offer guidance and encouragement. Consider joining a support group or attending workshops or therapy sessions specifically focused on overcoming limiting beliefs.

By using these techniques, you can begin to overcome your limiting beliefs and live a more fulfilling and authentic life. Remember that this is an ongoing process that requires persistence and patience, but the rewards of living a more fulfilling life are well worth the effort.

Do something!

Taking action is a crucial step in overcoming limiting beliefs. It's one thing to identify and challenge your limiting beliefs, but it's another to take the necessary steps to overcome them. In many cases, taking action can help you gain new experiences and perspectives, which can ultimately lead to a shift in your beliefs.

When you take action, you're not only challenging your limiting beliefs, but you're also building confidence in yourself and your abilities. Every time you take a step towards your goals, you're proving to yourself that you're capable of achieving them. Even if you encounter setbacks or failures along the way, you're still making progress and learning valuable lessons.

It's important to recognize that taking action doesn't always mean taking big, bold steps. Sometimes it can mean taking small, incremental steps towards your goals. This could involve setting achievable goals for yourself, breaking down larger goals into smaller, more manageable tasks, or simply trying new things and exploring different opportunities.

One effective way to take action is to create an action plan. This involves setting specific goals and outlining the steps you need to take to achieve them. When creating an action plan, it's important to be realistic and specific about what you want to achieve and what you need to do to get there.

Another important aspect of taking action is to stay motivated and persistent. It's easy to get discouraged when you encounter obstacles or setbacks, but it's important to stay focused on your goals and keep moving forward. Surrounding yourself with supportive people and resources can also help you stay motivated and on track.

- Remember that taking action is a process, and it may take time and effort to overcome your limiting beliefs. But by taking small, consistent steps towards your goals and staying committed to your vision, you can eventually break through your limiting beliefs and achieve the success and fulfillment you desire.
- Develop compassion for yourself.

Developing self-compassion is an essential component of overcoming limiting beliefs. It's easy to get frustrated or discouraged when trying to change deeply ingrained beliefs, but it's important to be patient and kind to yourself throughout the process.

Self-compassion involves treating yourself with the same kindness, concern, and understanding that you would offer to a good friend. This means acknowledging your struggles and limitations without judgment and offering yourself encouragement and support.

One effective way to develop self-compassion is to practice self-care. This involves taking care of your physical, emotional, and mental well-being by engaging in activities that nourish and recharge you. This could include exercise, meditation, spending time with loved ones, or pursuing hobbies and interests that bring you joy.

Another important aspect of self-compassion is to challenge negative self-talk. When you notice yourself engaging in self-criticism or negative self-talk, try to reframe those thoughts in a more positive and compassionate light. Instead of berating yourself for making mistakes or facing challenges, offer yourself words of encouragement and support.

It's also important to remember that self-compassion doesn't mean ignoring your problems or shortcomings. Instead, it involves approaching those challenges with kindness and understanding, and recognizing that you're doing the best you can with the resources and knowledge you have at the moment.

Developing self-compassion takes time and practice, but it can ultimately help you overcome limiting beliefs and live a more authentic and fulfilling life. By treating yourself with kindness and understanding, you can build resilience, boost your confidence, and develop a deeper sense of self-awareness and self-acceptance.

**Self-Aassessments Exercises.**

Self-assessment exercises are activities or tools that help individuals evaluate themselves in various areas of their lives, such as their strengths, weaknesses, values, goals, and overall well-being. These exercises can come in many forms, such as questionnaires, reflective writing prompts, or even simply taking time to reflect on one's experiences and feelings.

Self-assessment exercises can be beneficial in several ways. Firstly, they provide individuals with a clearer understanding of themselves and their needs, helping them make more informed decisions about their personal and professional lives. Secondly, they can help individuals identify areas for growth and improvement, which can lead to increased confidence, resilience, and adaptability. Finally, they can be a useful tool for goal setting, enabling individuals to establish concrete objectives and plans for achieving them.

Here are a few examples of self-assessment exercises that can help individuals improve their personal and professional lives:

1. Strengths assessment: This exercise involves reflecting on one's personal strengths and values. Individuals can use tools such as the VIA Character Strengths Survey or the StrengthsFinder assessment to identify their core strengths and how to leverage them to achieve their goals.

2. Goal-setting exercise: This exercise involves setting specific, measurable, achievable, relevant, and time-bound (SMART) goals. Individuals can break down their goals into smaller, achievable steps and track their progress along the way.

3. Values assessment: This exercise involves reflecting on one's core values and how they align with their personal and professional goals. Individuals can use tools such as the Personal Values Assessment to identify their values and ensure they are aligned with their actions and decisions.

4. Mindfulness meditation: This exercise involves taking time to focus on one's thoughts and feelings, and to cultivate a sense of present-moment awareness. Mindfulness meditation has been shown to reduce stress and anxiety, increase emotional resilience, and improve overall well-being.

5. Feedback exercise: This exercise involves seeking feedback from others on one's strengths, weaknesses, and areas for improvement. Individuals can use tools such as 360-degree feedback assessments or simply ask trusted friends, family members, or colleagues for their honest feedback.

6. Journaling: This exercise involves reflecting on one's experiences and emotions through writing. Journaling can help individuals identify patterns in their behaviour and emotions, clarify their thoughts and feelings, and track their progress over time.

Self-assessment exercises can be a valuable tool for personal and professional growth and development. By taking the time to reflect on one's strengths, weaknesses, values, and goals, individuals can gain a clearer understanding of themselves and their needs and develop a plan for achieving their objectives.

## The Advantages of Self-Evaluation Exercises.

Exercises in self-assessment can assist people in many ways. They first aid people in developing a deeper awareness of themselves. Self-assessment exercises enable people to gain understanding of their personalities, strengths, weaknesses, and values. Self-awareness is a crucial component of personal development. People can make wise judgments regarding their personal and professional life by developing a greater awareness of themselves.

Second, self-assessment exercises assist people in identifying areas that require development. Individuals can identify areas where they need to improve and create a strategy to do so by assessing their own performance. This can be particularly helpful for individuals who are trying to develop their careers, since they can identify the skills and competences required for their chosen roles.

Thirdly, self-evaluation exercises aid in goal setting and progress monitoring. By assessing their talents and shortcomings, individuals can set realistic goals and develop a plan to attain them. Self-assessment exercises also enable people to monitor their progress toward their objectives and change as necessary.

Fourthly, self-assessment exercises can improve relationships. When individuals have a greater awareness of their own strengths and weaknesses, they can communicate better with others and develop stronger relationships. They can also identify their own biases and prejudices, and work to address them. This can lead to greater empathy, understanding, and collaboration with others.

Fifthly, self-assessment exercises can enhance decision-making skills. When individuals have a deeper understanding of their own values and priorities, they can make decisions that align with these values. This can lead to greater satisfaction and a sense of purpose in one's life.

Finally, self-assessment exercises can help individuals to take ownership of their own personal growth and development. By identifying areas for improvement and setting goals, individuals can take control of their own lives and actively work towards self-improvement. This can lead to greater confidence, self-esteem, and a sense of accomplishment.

Overall, self-assessment exercises can be a valuable tool for personal growth and development. They can help individuals gain self-awareness, identify areas for improvement, set goals, and take ownership of their own growth. By regularly engaging in self-assessment, individuals can continue to grow and develop throughout their lives.

**Self-Assessment Exercise Examples.**

Here are a few examples of self-assessment exercises that can be helpful:

1. Personality assessments: Personality assessments, such as the Myers-Briggs Type Indicator (MBTI) and the Big Five Personality Traits, can help individuals gain a better understanding of their personality traits, including their strengths and weaknesses.
2. 360-degree feedback surveys: These surveys gather feedback from a variety of sources, including colleagues, managers, and subordinates, to provide a comprehensive view of an individual's performance and areas for improvement.

3. Goal-setting exercises: Goal-setting exercises can assist individuals in identifying and defining their objectives, as well as developing a plan to achieve them. The SMART goal-setting framework is a popular method for setting specific, measurable, achievable, relevant, and time-bound goals.

4. Skills assessments: Skills assessments can help individuals identify their strengths and areas where they may need improvement. These assessments can be used to develop a plan for building new skills or enhancing existing ones.

5. Reflection exercises: Reflection exercises, such as journaling or meditation, can help individuals gain a deeper understanding of their thoughts and feelings. This self-awareness can aid in personal growth and development.

By using self-assessment exercises, individuals can gain valuable insights into their personal growth and development, identify areas for improvement, and develop strategies to achieve their goals. These exercises can also aid in the development of self-awareness and self-confidence.

**Evaluation of Strengths and Weaknesses.**

1. Personal Values Assessment Another self-assessment exercise is to evaluate one's personal values. This entails considering what is most important to oneself in life and what principles guide one's behaviour. People can do this by reflecting on questions like:

 • What matters to me most in life?

 • What principles or beliefs do I stand for?

 • What do I want to be remembered for? By assessing one's personal values, individuals can gain a greater understanding of themselves and their priorities, which can help guide decision-making and goal setting.

2. Career Assessment Individuals can also use self-assessment exercises to evaluate their career goals and progress. This can involve identifying one's strengths, interests, and skills, as well as researching potential career paths and opportunities. People can do this by asking questions like: • What are my strengths and skills? • What career paths align with my interests and values? • What steps can I take to achieve my career goals? By conducting a career assessment, individuals can gain clarity on their career aspirations and develop a plan to pursue them.

3. Emotional Intelligence Assessment Emotional intelligence (EI) refers to the ability to identify, understand, and manage one's own emotions, as well as the emotions of others. Self-assessment exercises can help individuals evaluate their own emotional intelligence and identify areas where they can improve. People can do this by reflecting on questions like:

4. • How well do I manage my own emotions?

5. • How well do I understand the emotions of others?

6. • How do I respond to challenging situations? By assessing their emotional intelligence, individuals can enhance their self-awareness and develop skills to improve their relationships with others.

7. Time Management Assessment Effective time management is essential for personal and professional success. Self-assessment exercises can help individuals evaluate their own time management skills and identify areas for improvement. People can do this by reflecting on questions like:

How do I prioritize tasks and activities?

- How do I manage distractions and interruptions?

- How do I balance work and personal life?

By assessing their time management skills, individuals can develop strategies to maximize their productivity and achieve their goals more efficiently.

Overall, self-assessment exercises can help individuals gain a deeper understanding of themselves and their goals, as well as identify areas where they can improve. By regularly engaging in self-assessment, individuals can develop a plan for personal and professional growth and achieve greater success and fulfillment in their lives.

Those who evaluate their emotional intelligence can learn more about how well they are able to control their emotions and create a plan to become more emotionally intelligent.

8.  Feedback Evaluation

An exercise in self-evaluation known as a feedback assessment involves asking for feedback from others to measure our performance, competencies, and capabilities. This activity might be especially beneficial for people who desire to advance their professions and their skill sets.

Individuals can accomplish this by asking co-workers, acquaintances, or family members for feedback on their work, abilities, and skills. Individuals can identify areas that require improvement and create a strategy to address them by assessing the input.

Self-evaluation exercises are crucial for personal development, to sum up. They aid people in understanding their personalities, traits, flaws, values, and aptitudes. Individuals can identify areas that need improvement and create a strategy to reach their objectives by examining their performance, skills, and talents.

Self-assessment exercises can assist people in making educated decisions about their personal and professional lives, whether it is by analysing our time management abilities, emotional intelligence, or career aspirations.

Individuals can learn more about their job ambitions and create a strategy to accomplish them by responding to these questions.

# Chapter Six

## RECOGNIZING AND EMBRACING PERSONAL STRENGTHS AND WEAKNESSES

A crucial part of personal growth and development is self-authentication, which is the process of recognizing and validating one's true self. Much more, an important component of self-authentication is acknowledging and accepting one's own strengths and weakness.

In this chapter, we'll talk about why it's important to be aware of your own strengths and weaknesses, how to do it, and how to use that information to live a more fulfilling life.

Why Is It Necessary to Recognize One's Own Strengths and Weaknesses?

Understanding the importance of identifying one's own strengths and weaknesses is the first step in the process. Knowing your assets and liabilities is the cornerstone of self-awareness.

Understanding your own feelings, ideas, and behaviours as well as how they affect you and other people is known as self-awareness. This information is essential for your personal growth and development since it enables you to see your strengths and places for improvement.

Knowing your assets enables you to take advantage of them, which can boost your self-assurance and self-esteem. Also, it can assist you in locating employment that plays to your skills, which can increase job success and job satisfaction.

Finding your shortcomings is equally important because it gives insight into areas where you might need to put in more effort or seek assistance. You may create tactics to go past your limitations and transform them into strengths by being aware of them.

**Advantages of Understanding and Accepting Your Limitations and Strengths**

- Improved Self-Awareness

Those who are more aware of their own strengths and flaws are better able to understand their emotions, thoughts, and behaviours. Self-awareness enables people to identify their shortcomings and growth areas. This information promotes higher personal development.

- Improved Relationships

Partnerships improve when people are aware of their own talents and flaws. Individuals are better able to recognize the strengths and shortcomings of others when they are aware of their own weaknesses. Relationships become healthier and more fulfilling as a result of this understanding, which fosters a more sympathetic and empathetic view of others.

- Self-confidence

Self-confidence is boosted by an awareness of one's personal assets and flaws. It aids people in recognizing their special skills and capabilities, which raises self-esteem. Those who possess this confidence can pursue their hobbies and aspirations without worrying about failing.

- Improved Decision-Making

Acknowledging one's own advantages and disadvantages improves decision-making. Individuals are better able to make decisions that fit their capabilities and constraints when they are aware of their strengths and weaknesses. This understanding leads to improved outcomes and minimizes the risk of failure.

**How to Determine Your Own Strengths and Weaknesses.**

Finding one's own unique strengths and shortcomings might be difficult because many of us are unfamiliar with thinking about ourselves in this way. To assist you determine your strengths and shortcomings, you can use a number of tactics, including:

- Self – Assessment Exercises: Self-assessment exercises can be found online, and they can be used to help you determine your strengths and limitations. Usually, after answering a series of questions, you receive a report outlining your strengths and limitations.

- Request Input from Others: Receiving feedback from others is a great approach to learn more about your skills and limitations. You can enlist the help of close friends, relatives, or co-workers to give you constructive criticism on your strengths and faults.

- Consider Your Past Experiences: Considering your previous experiences might also assist you in determining your strengths and limitations. Consider both your successful and unsuccessful periods. What elements played a part in your success or failure?

- Maintain a Journal: Keeping a journal can help you better understand your strengths and shortcomings by allowing you to record your ideas and experiences. This might assist you in identifying behavioural and mental patterns that can be influencing your strengths and shortcomings.

## Utilizing Personal Strengths and Weaknesses.

The next stage is to apply what you've learned about your personal talents and limitations to live a more fulfilling life. These are some strategies for maximizing your attributes and improving your weaknesses:

- Find methods to harness your abilities in both your personal and professional life to make the most of them. For instance, if you have a great ability to communicate, look for chances to do so with others.

- Work on Your Weaknesses: Make a list of tactics you can use to get over them. For instance, if you have trouble managing your time, make a timetable to make it easier for you to do so.

- Get Support: Ask for help from others if you are having trouble with a particular weakness. This can entail asking a mentor, coach, or therapist for advice.

- Utilize your understanding of your skills and shortcomings to help you set reasonable goals for yourself. Establish objectives that capitalize on your advantages and push you to strengthen your weaknesses.

**Self-Authentication Through Understanding of Personal Strengths and Weaknesses.**

- Create a Growth Mindset:

The first step in creating a growth mindset is recognizing one's own strengths and flaws. A growth mentality is the conviction that talents can develop with commitment and effort. It enables people to take on difficulties and see failure as a chance to improve.

- Accept Imperfection

Individuals can accept imperfection by being aware of their own strengths and weaknesses. People can concentrate on their strengths while acknowledging their flaws when they accept imperfection. This way of thinking enables people to take chances and go after their dreams while lowering their fear of failure.

- Focus on Personal Development

Personal growth comes from identifying one's personal assets and weaknesses. Personal development entails gaining information and skills to enhance one's quality of life. Maximizing one's potential through personal development results in a more fulfilling existence.

- Be Yourself

Being Yourself involves being aware of your own advantages and disadvantages. Being authentic is staying true to who you are and acting in accordance with your values and beliefs. Individuals can be authentic by accepting both their strengths and shortcomings, which promotes more self-assurance, self-awareness, and self-acceptance.

Being real, keeping loyal to oneself, and adhering to one's principles and convictions are all aspects of living authentically. It entails being loyal to one's own wants and objectives, accepting oneself for who we are, and being honest with oneself. Although real living is difficult, it is necessary for a happy life. In this piece, we'll talk about the value of living genuinely and offer some advice on how to achieve it.

# Chapter Seven

## LIVING AUTHENTICALLY

**What does it entail to live an authentic life?**

Living authentically also means taking responsibility for your own life and making choices that are aligned with your values and beliefs. It involves being honest with yourself and others and expressing your true feelings and opinions. It means accepting and embracing your strengths and weaknesses, and not pretending to be someone you're not.

In essence, living authentically means being true to yourself and living a life that is meaningful and fulfilling to you, rather than trying to conform to societal expectations or the expectations of others. It may require courage and vulnerability, but the rewards of living authentically can be immense, including a sense of purpose, contentment, and inner peace.

It entails refraining from acting disingenuously to blend in or win favour with others. Living an authentic life means following your deepest dreams and objectives.

The significance of living authentically

living authentically is vital because it allows us to build deeper relationships, make wiser choices, and experience a sense of contentment and happiness in our lives. It requires us to be truthful with ourselves about our identity, convictions, and values and to refrain from acting inauthentically to please others. While the process of self-discovery and authentic living can be challenging, it ultimately leads to a more fulfilling and satisfying life.

**Advice for living an authentic life.**

Living an authentic life is one of the most fulfilling and rewarding experiences one can have. It is a process that requires self-awareness, honesty, and courage. To help you on your journey to authenticity my advice is to be true to yourself, even if it means being different: It's easy to fall into the trap of conforming to the norms of society or following the crowd. But living authentically requires us to embrace our unique qualities and stand out from the crowd. As Oscar Wilde once said, "Be yourself; everyone else is already taken."

1.  Don't be afraid to make mistakes: Living an authentic life means taking risks and making mistakes. Don't let the fear of failure hold you back from pursuing your dreams and living life on your own terms. As author Neil Gaiman once said, "The one thing that you have that nobody else has is you. Your voice, your mind, your

story, your vision. So write and draw and build and play and dance and live as only you can."

2. Take time to reflect on your values and beliefs: To live an authentic life, it's important to understand what you stand for and what matters to you. Take time to reflect on your values and beliefs, and make sure your actions align with them. As philosopher Socrates once said, "The unexamined life is not worth living."

3. Surround yourself with supportive people: Living authentically can be challenging, so it's important to have a support system of people who accept and encourage you for who you are. Surround yourself with people who share your values and support your dreams. As author Maya Angelou once said, "I've learned that people will forget what you said, people will forget what you did, but people will never forget how you made them feel."

4. Practice self-care: Living an authentic life means being true to yourself, but it's also important to take care of yourself physically, emotionally, and mentally. Make time for activities that bring you joy, practice self-compassion, and prioritize your well-being.

5. Embrace vulnerability: Living authentically means being vulnerable and exposing your true self to the world. Embrace vulnerability as a strength, not a weakness, and allow yourself to be seen and heard. As author Brené Brown once said, "Vulnerability is the birthplace of love, belonging, joy, courage, empathy, and creativity. It is the source of hope, empathy, accountability, and authenticity."

6. Learn to say no: Living an authentic life means setting boundaries and saying no to things that don't align with your values or bring you joy. Don't be afraid to say no to people or opportunities that don't serve your authentic self. As author Elizabeth Gilbert once said, "Saying no is a complete sentence. It does not require justification or explanation."

7. Take action towards your dreams: Living an authentic life means pursuing your dreams and passions. Don't let fear or self-doubt hold you back from taking action towards your goals. As author Paulo Coelho once said, "When you want something, all the universe conspires in helping you to achieve it."

8. Practice gratitude: Living authentically means being grateful for the blessings in your life and acknowledging the challenges that have shaped you. Practice gratitude daily and focus on the positive aspects of your life. As author Melody Beattie once said, "Gratitude unlocks the fullness of life. It turns what we have into enough, and more. It turns denial into acceptance, chaos to order, confusion to clarity. It can turn a meal into a feast, a house into a home, a stranger into a friend."

9. Remember that authenticity is not only a journey, but also an adventure!

**Choose your ideals and principles.**

Finding your values and beliefs is the first step towards living authentically. Spend some time considering what matters most to you in life. What central beliefs guide you? What do you hold true? Put them in writing and use them frequently.

Be truthful to yourself.

Being truthful to oneself is a crucial aspect of living authentically. It means accepting and acknowledging all aspects of yourself, including your flaws and weaknesses. It can be difficult to confront parts of ourselves that we don't like or want to change, but accepting and owning them can lead to a sense of inner peace and authenticity. It's also important to be honest about your desires and aspirations, and to pursue them even if they don't align with societal norms or expectations. By being truthful to yourself, you can live a life that is consistent with your values and beliefs, and ultimately feel more fulfilled and content.

Never assess yourself against others.

When we focus too much on comparing ourselves to others, we can lose sight of our own unique journey and what makes us special. Instead of trying to live up to someone else's standards or expectations, it's important to embrace our own strengths and weaknesses, and strive to be the best version of ourselves that we can be.

By setting our own goals and standards, we can focus on personal growth and development, rather than trying to measure up to someone else's achievements or success. It's also important to remember that success is not a one-size-fits-all concept, and what may be considered success for one person may not be the same for another. By staying true to our own values and beliefs, we can define success on our own terms and find fulfillment in our own unique way.

So, instead of comparing ourselves to others, let's focus on our own journey and celebrate our own accomplishments and strengths. Let's embrace our uniqueness and live authentically, without the need to conform or fit in with societal expectations. By doing so, we can lead a more fulfilling and satisfying life.

Be surrounded by encouraging individuals.

Surrounding yourself with supportive and encouraging individuals is essential for living an authentic life. Being around people who accept and value you for who you are can help you feel more comfortable and confident in expressing your true self. On the other hand, being around people who constantly criticize or judge you can create feelings of insecurity and self-doubt, leading you to hide your true identity or conform to societal expectations.

When looking for supportive people, seek out those who share similar values and beliefs, and who encourage you to pursue your passions and goals. It's also important to remember that relationships are a two-way street, so make sure to offer support and encouragement to those around you as well.

If you find yourself surrounded by people who are not supportive or who pressure you to be someone you're not, it may be time to re-evaluate those relationships and make changes as necessary. It can be difficult to let go of toxic relationships, but in the long run, it is better for your mental and emotional well-being to surround yourself with people who bring out the best in you and support your authentic self.

Do something!

Living your truth is one of the most critical aspects of leading an authentic life. It entails being truthful to oneself and living in accordance with one's beliefs and principles, regardless of what others may think or say. Living in this manner can help you achieve your aspirations, be content with your choices, and feel a sense of purpose and meaning in your life.

One of the most important reasons why it is essential to live your truth is that it can help you achieve your goals. When you live in accordance with your values and beliefs, you are more likely to make choices that will take you in the direction of your objectives. You will feel more motivated and committed to working towards your aspirations since you will be acting in a manner that is consistent with your values and beliefs.

Additionally, living your truth can help you be more content with your choices. When you make choices that are true to who you are and what you believe in, you are less likely to have regrets or second-guess your decisions. You will be able to embrace the consequences of your choices and take ownership of them, knowing that they are a reflection of your genuine self.

Living your truth can also give your life a sense of purpose and meaning. When you live in accordance with your values and principles, you will feel more connected to your inner self, which will help you feel a greater sense of fulfillment and satisfaction. You will be able to identify your goals and aspirations more clearly, as well as work towards achieving them with a sense of purpose.

So, how can you approach living your truth in the best way possible? The first step is to identify your values and beliefs. Reflect on what is truly important to you and what you stand for. Consider the experiences that have shaped your beliefs and principles and what you have learned from them. Write down your values and beliefs and try to be as clear and specific as possible.

Once you have identified your values and beliefs, the next step is to commit to living in accordance with them. This means making choices that are consistent with your values and beliefs, even if they may be difficult or unpopular. It means being true to who you are, regardless of what others may think or say.

To help you live your truth, it is essential to be confident in yourself and your beliefs. This does not mean being arrogant or closed-minded, but rather having the courage to stand up for what you believe in and being open to learning and growing. Be willing to take risks and try new things but do so in a manner that is consistent with your values and beliefs.

It is also helpful to surround yourself with people who support and encourage you to live your truth. This can be friends, family, or a supportive community that shares your values and beliefs. These individuals can provide you with the guidance, feedback, and encouragement you need to stay true to yourself and achieve your goals.

Finally, remember that living your truth is an ongoing process. It requires continual self-reflection, growth, and learning. Be patient with yourself and be open to making mistakes and learning from them. Living your truth is not always easy, but it is always worth the effort.

Living your truth is one of the most critical aspects of leading an authentic life. It can help you achieve your goals, be content with your choices, and feel a sense of purpose and meaning in your life. By identifying your values and beliefs, committing to living in accordance with them, surrounding yourself with supportive individuals, and being confident in yourself and your beliefs, you can approach living your truth in the best way possible. Remember that living your truth is a continual process that requires ongoing self-reflection, growth, and learning.

When we know who we are and what we stand for, it's time to take action. Action is an essential aspect of living an authentic life. It's not enough to simply know our beliefs and values; we must put them into practice in our daily lives. Without taking action, our convictions remain just that: beliefs without the power to transform us and the world around us.

So, how can we approach doing something that aligns with our beliefs and values? Here are some tips:

1.  Start small: It's easy to get overwhelmed by the enormity of the changes we want to make in our lives. Start by taking small steps towards your goals. These small steps build momentum and help us gain confidence in our ability to take action.

2.  Set achievable goals: It's important to set goals that are achievable. This means being realistic about what we can accomplish and setting targets that we can reach with hard work and dedication.

3.  Be consistent: Consistency is key to achieving any goal. It's important to make a habit of doing something every day that aligns with our beliefs and values. This helps us stay committed and focused on our goals.

4.  Surround yourself with supportive people: Surrounding ourselves with people who share our values and beliefs is important. These people can provide us with support, encouragement, and accountability.

5.  Take risks: Living an authentic life often means taking risks. We must be willing to step outside our comfort zone and take chances if we want to achieve our goals.

6.  Learn from failure: Failure is a natural part of the process of taking action. We must be willing to learn from our mistakes and failures and use them as opportunities for growth and improvement.

7.  Stay true to yourself: Finally, it's important to stay true to ourselves and our values. We must not compromise our principles in order to fit in or please others. Living an authentic life means being true to ourselves, even when it's difficult or unpopular.

Taking action that aligns with our beliefs and values can be a daunting task, but it's essential to living an authentic life. It requires courage, commitment, and perseverance.

By starting small, setting achievable goals, being consistent, surrounding ourselves with supportive people, taking risks, learning from failure, and staying true to ourselves, we can take action that transforms our lives and the world around us.

**Accept change.**

Let's face it, change can be a scary thing. It's like when you finally get used to the way your hair looks and then your stylist suggests a new haircut. But, as scary as it may be, change is necessary for living an authentic life.

Think about it, if you never try anything new or different, how will you ever know what you truly enjoy or what you're capable of? Change can open up new doors and opportunities that you never even knew existed.

Plus, living genuinely requires change. You can't expect to grow and become the person you were meant to be if you're stuck in the same old routine. It's like trying to fit into the jeans you wore in high school - it's just not going to happen. Well, not for me anyway. You need to embrace change and be willing to adapt to new situations and experiences.

Now, don't get me wrong, change can be uncomfortable and even painful at times. It's like wearing shoes that are a size too small - it hurts, but eventually you adjust, and they become your new normal. Similarly, change may be uncomfortable at first, but as you adapt, it becomes a part of who you are.

And let's not forget about the benefits of change. Trying new things and stepping out of your comfort zone can lead to personal growth and development. It's like going to the gym - it may be tough at first, but as you continue to push yourself, you become stronger and more resilient.

So, don't be afraid of change. Embrace it, welcome it, and see where it takes you. You never know, it may just lead you down a path of self-discovery and fulfillment. And who knows, maybe that new haircut will be your new signature look.

**Building Supportive Relationships and Communities.**

Creating communities and relationships that support one another is an essential component of self-authentication. Without a supportive environment, individuals may struggle to understand, accept, and affirm their genuine identities. Moreover, self-authentication is a process that requires a strong foundation of self-awareness, self-acceptance, and self-love, all of which can be fostered through supportive relationships and communities.

Think about it. When you are surrounded by individuals who accept and appreciate you for who you are, it becomes easier to be honest with yourself about your strengths and weaknesses. You can let go of the pressure to be someone you're not and instead embrace your unique qualities, quirks, and idiosyncrasies. You begin to see yourself as a complete individual, with your own set of experiences, perspectives, and goals.

However, without supportive relationships and communities, individuals may struggle to understand their genuine identities. When we are surrounded by individuals who don't accept us for who we are, we may begin to question our worth and value. We may feel like we have to hide or suppress parts of ourselves in order to fit in or be accepted. This can lead to feelings of loneliness, isolation, and disconnection, which can take a toll on our mental health and overall well-being.

Moreover, self-authentication is a process that requires a strong foundation of self-awareness, self-acceptance, and self-love. When we have supportive relationships and communities, we are more likely to develop these qualities. Supportive relationships and communities can provide a safe space for individuals to explore and understand their true selves. They can also offer validation and affirmation, which can be crucial for individuals who may have struggled with self-doubt or self-criticism in the past.

Developing supportive relationships and communities can support self-authentication by:

1.  Encouraging Self-Exploration: Supportive relationships and communities can provide a safe space for individuals to explore and understand their true selves. This can involve reflecting on past experiences, identifying core values and beliefs, and setting personal goals. When individuals feel comfortable exploring these aspects of themselves, they are more likely to gain a deeper understanding of their genuine identities.

2.  Offering Validation and Affirmation: Validation and affirmation are essential components of self-acceptance and self-love. Supportive relationships and communities can offer validation and affirmation for individuals' unique qualities, experiences, and perspectives. This can help individuals build a positive self-image and feel more confident in themselves and their abilities.

3.  Providing Direction and Encouragement: Supportive relationships and communities can also provide direction and encouragement for individuals as they navigate the process of self-authentication. This can involve setting achievable goals, offering guidance and feedback, and celebrating successes along the way. When individuals have a support system that encourages and motivates them, they are more likely to stay committed to their personal growth and development.

But what does it mean to create supportive relationships and communities? How can individuals go about developing these types of relationships and communities?

Here are some techniques that can support the process of self-authentication:

1. Find Like-Minded Individuals: Finding individuals who share similar values, interests, or experiences can be an excellent way to develop supportive relationships and communities. This can involve joining clubs or organizations, attending events, or even using social media to connect with individuals who share your interests.

2. Build Trust: Trust is a crucial component of supportive relationships and communities. Individuals need to feel like they can be themselves without judgment or criticism. This can involve being vulnerable and honest with others and offering the same level of trust and respect in return.

3. Practice Active Listening: Active listening involves being fully present and engaged in conversations with others. This can involve asking questions, offering feedback, and being open to different perspectives

**Make a list of your values and pursuits!**

Making a list of your values and pursuits is like setting a compass for your life. It helps you stay on course and navigate the choppy waters of existence with a sense of purpose and direction. But let's be real, making lists can be a real snooze-fest. So let's spice things up a bit and make it fun!

First of all, don't just make a boring old list. Get creative! Maybe you want to create a vision board, where you can visually represent your values and pursuits with pictures, quotes, and symbols. Or perhaps you'd rather write a song or poem about your values and what they mean to you. Whatever medium you choose, make it something that speaks to your soul and makes you feel inspired.

Now, let's talk about values. What are they exactly? Well, values are the guiding principles that shape our lives and define who we are as individuals. They can be things like honesty, integrity, compassion, courage, or creativity. The beauty of values is that they're unique to each person. What's important to you may not be important to someone else, and that's okay. Embrace your values and own them!

When making your list of values, think about what matters most to you. What do you stand for? What do you want to be known for? What are the non-negotiables in your life? These are the values that will guide your decisions and actions, even when the going gets tough.

Now, let's move on to pursuits. Pursuits are the things that make us come alive. They're our passions, hobbies, and interests. Pursuits are important because they bring joy and fulfillment to our lives. They're the things that make us feel alive and connected to something greater than ourselves.

When making your list of pursuits, don't be afraid to dream big! Maybe you've always wanted to learn how to play guitar or start your own business. Maybe you want to travel the world or write a book. Whatever your pursuits may be, write them down and make a plan to pursue them.

The key to making your values and pursuits a reality is to take action. Don't just make a list and forget about it. Use it as a roadmap for your life and take steps every day to live in alignment with your values and pursue your passions. Surround yourself with people who support you and inspire you to be your best self.

Making a list of your values and pursuits doesn't have to be boring. Get creative and have fun with it! Remember, your values and pursuits are what make you unique and special.

Embrace them and own them. Use them as a compass to guide your life and make your dreams a reality.

**Look for different viewpoints.**

Oh wow, looking for different viewpoints is like opening a treasure chest filled with unique and intriguing ideas! It's like discovering a new flavour of ice cream or stumbling upon a hidden gem in a thrift store. It's an adventure that can take you to unexpected places and broaden your horizons.

But before we dive into the benefits of seeking out different viewpoints, let's define what we mean by "viewpoints." A viewpoint is a person's unique perspective or opinion on a particular topic or issue. It's influenced by their life experiences, beliefs, and values. No two people have the exact same viewpoint, which is what makes seeking them out so valuable.

Now, let's talk about why seeking out different viewpoints is so important. First and foremost, it helps you challenge your assumptions and beliefs. We all have our own biases and preconceived notions about the world, but when we expose ourselves to different perspectives, we're forced to re-examine those beliefs. It's like cleaning out your closet and getting rid of clothes you haven't worn in years - it creates space for new ideas and perspectives to enter your mind.

Seeking out different viewpoints can also help you develop empathy and understanding. When we're exposed to different experiences and perspectives, we start to realize that our own worldview isn't the only valid one. This can help us become more compassionate and empathetic towards others, which in turn can strengthen our relationships and communities.

Speaking of relationships, seeking out different viewpoints is a great way to make new connections with people. When we only surround ourselves with people who think and act like us, we limit our potential for growth and connection. By seeking out diverse viewpoints, we can connect with people from different backgrounds and experiences, which can enrich our lives and broaden our social circles.

But how can we actually seek out different viewpoints? Well, it's easier than you might think. Here are a few ideas to get you started:

1.  Read books and articles from different perspectives. If you typically read books and articles from authors who share your beliefs and values, challenge yourself to read something from a different perspective. You might be surprised by what you learn!
2.  Attend events and talks on topics you're interested in, but from different perspectives. For example, if you're interested in politics, attend a talk from a politician or political commentator who holds different views than you.
3.  Engage in conversations with people who have different viewpoints. This can be tricky, as it requires you to approach the conversation with an open mind and a willingness to listen. But if you can do it, you'll likely come away with a deeper understanding of the issue at hand.
4.  Join groups or organizations that focus on diversity and inclusion. These groups are designed to bring together people from different backgrounds and perspectives and can be a great way to make new connections and learn from others.

Seeking out different viewpoints is like adding a new flavour to your life - it can be a bit scary at first, but ultimately, it's worth it. By challenging our assumptions, developing empathy, and understanding, and making new connections, we can enrich our lives and build stronger, more diverse communities. So go ahead, open that treasure chest and see what amazing ideas and perspectives you can discover!

**Be open-minded and sincere!**

Being open and honest with others can be scary. It means putting yourself out there, warts and all, and hoping that the people around you will still accept you. But the thing is, when we're open and honest with others, we give them permission to be open and honest with us. And that's when the real magic happens.

Think about it: have you ever been in a situation where you felt like you couldn't be yourself around someone? Maybe you were afraid of being judged or rejected. How did that feel? Not great, right? On the other hand, have you ever been around someone who just seemed so comfortable in their own skin that it made you feel more comfortable too? That's the power of vulnerability.

When we're open and honest with others, we create a space where people can be themselves. We create a space where people can share their fears, their hopes, their dreams, and their struggles. And when we do that, we create real connections with others.

But let's be real: vulnerability is not always easy. It can be scary to let people see the real you. So, how do we become more open-minded and sincere? Here are a few tips:

1.  Practice self-acceptance: Before you can be open and honest with others, you need to be open and honest with yourself. Accept your flaws, your imperfections, and your quirks. Be kind to yourself, even when you mess up. When you can accept yourself, it becomes easier to be open with others.

2. Start small: You don't have to spill your deepest secrets to everyone you meet. Start by sharing something small with someone you trust. Maybe it's a fear you have or a struggle you're going through. When you see that the other person accepts you for who you are, it becomes easier to open up more.

3. Listen: Being open-minded and sincere isn't just about sharing your own thoughts and feelings. It's also about listening to others. When someone shares something with you, really listen. Don't judge, don't try to fix, just be present with them.

4. Be patient: Being vulnerable is a process. It takes time and practice. Don't beat yourself up if you're not perfect at it right away. Keep trying, keep practicing, and you'll get there.

5. Laugh: Okay, this might not seem like it belongs on a list of tips for being open-minded and sincere but hear me out. Sometimes, the best way to connect with others is through laughter. When we can laugh at ourselves and our own quirks, it creates a sense of shared humanity with others. So, don't take yourself too seriously. Have a little fun.

So, there you have it. Being open-minded and sincere isn't always easy, but it's worth it. When we're open and honest with ourselves and others, we create deep and meaningful connections with those around us. And that's what life is all about, isn't it?

**Use your active listening skills.**

Hmmm, active listening - it's like the holy grail of communication skills! And let's be honest, we could all use a little more active listening in our lives. After all, how often do we really give someone our undivided attention without distractions, interruptions, or judgment? Not very often, I'd wager. But fear not, my friend, for I am here to help you become a master of active listening!

First things first, let's define what active listening is. Essentially, it's a way of listening to someone that involves giving them your full attention, acknowledging their perspective, and responding in a way that shows you understand what they're saying. It's about creating a space where the other person feels heard, valued, and respected.

So, why is active listening so important? Well, for starters, it helps to build stronger relationships with others. When we actively listen to someone, we're showing them that we care about what they have to say and that we value their input. This can lead to deeper connections, increased trust, and better communication overall.

Plus, active listening can help to prevent misunderstandings and conflicts. When we take the time to really listen to someone, we're less likely to jump to conclusions or make assumptions about what they mean. We're also more likely to pick up on subtle nuances in their communication that we might otherwise miss. This can help to prevent misunderstandings and ensure that everyone is on the same page.

So, how do you become an active listener? Well, it takes a little bit of practice, but it's definitely achievable. Here are some tips to get you started:

1.  Give the person your full attention: When someone is speaking to you, put down your phone, turn off the TV, and really focus on what they're saying. Give them your full attention and make eye contact to show that you're engaged in the conversation.
2.  Avoid interrupting or passing judgment: It can be tempting to jump in with your own thoughts or opinions but try to resist the urge to interrupt. Instead, let the person finish what they're saying before responding. And avoid passing judgment or making assumptions about what they mean.

3. Clarify and summarize: To show that you're really listening, try to summarize what the person has said in your own words. This can help to ensure that you've understood their message correctly. And if you're not sure what they mean, ask for clarification.

4. Show empathy: If the person is sharing something personal or emotional, show empathy by acknowledging their feelings and validating their experience. This can help to create a deeper connection and show that you care.

5. Respond thoughtfully: When it's your turn to speak, respond thoughtfully and respectfully. Acknowledge the person's perspective and offer your own thoughts or opinions in a constructive way.

So there you have it - a crash course in active listening! With a little practice, you can become a master of this crucial communication skill and build deeper connections with those around you. So go forth and listen actively, my friend!

Provide assistance and inspiration to others.

And let's not forget the warm fuzzy feeling that comes with helping others! Being a source of assistance and inspiration to those around you is not only beneficial for them but also for your own well-being. It's a win-win situation.

Think about the last time someone helped you when you needed it the most. Didn't it feel amazing to have someone by your side, supporting you and encouraging you to keep going? By being that same support for others, you can make a positive impact on their lives and build strong, meaningful connections.

But being a source of assistance and inspiration doesn't mean you have to be a superhero or have all the answers. Sometimes, just being there to listen and offer a kind word can make all the difference. It's about showing that you care and are willing to help in any way you can.

And let's not forget the power of celebrating others' accomplishments. When someone achieves something great, it's important to acknowledge and celebrate their success. This can be as simple as sending a congratulatory message or sharing their success with others. By doing so, you're not only showing support for that individual, but also spreading positivity and inspiring others to reach for their own goals.

So, don't underestimate the impact you can have on those around you by providing assistance and inspiration. It's a small but powerful way to create a more supportive and authentic community.

**Setting limits.**

Setting limits is crucial for creating communities and supporting connections. Being upfront about your wants, expectations, and restrictions in relationships is what it means to set boundaries. It entails setting clear limits between yourself and others and upholding them when necessary.

Establishing boundaries can help you establish good relationships, safeguard your mental and emotional health, and provide your connections a sense of safety and security.

**Develope gratitude.**

It is crucial to practice appreciation in order to create empowering connections and communities. Being grateful for the people and experiences in your life and showing that thankfulness to others is what it means to be grateful.

Focusing on the positive parts of your relationships and appreciating those who support and encourage you on your road toward self-authentication can both be aided by cultivating thankfulness.

## Setting Boundaries and Saying No.

Setting boundaries and learning to say no are essential components of living an authentic life. Boundaries are essentially rules that individuals establish to decide what activities, relationships, and behaviours are appropriate or inappropriate based on their own values and ideas. Saying no, on the other hand, means turning down requests or opportunities that do not align with one's own goals, passions, or values. Both of these actions help individuals develop a sense of independence, self-respect, and self-awareness, all of which are crucial for self-authenticity.

One of the key benefits of defining boundaries is the ability to clearly define limits for one's own behaviour and relationships with others. When individuals are clear about what they will and will not tolerate, they are better able to communicate their wants and expectations to others and avoid situations that could lead to conflict or stress. This can be especially important in interpersonal relationships, where misunderstandings and miscommunications often lead to hurt feelings, resentment, and even more serious disputes.

Defining limits can also help individuals assert their particular values and priorities. When individuals are clear about their own beliefs and principles, they are better able to recognize situations and interactions that are at odds with those values. They can then take appropriate action to stand up for their principles and put their own integrity first rather than compromising those principles for the sake of others.

Saying no is also a crucial component of self-authenticity because it enables individuals to put their own objectives, interests, and values first. When individuals refuse opportunities or requests that conflict with their personal priorities, they maintain a sense of autonomy and self-determination. This can be especially important in situations where individuals may feel pressured to fulfill social expectations or standards, or to take on tasks or roles that do not reflect their own values or aspirations.

Saying no can also help individuals avoid burnout and overwhelm by preventing them from accepting too many responsibilities or commitments. Many individuals may feel obligated to accept every invitation or opportunity that presents itself out of a sense of duty or a fear of missing out. However, this often leads to overcommitment and living a life that is out of balance. By saying no to some requests or opportunities, individuals can put their own wellbeing first and ensure they have the time and energy to focus on the things that mean the most to them.

In addition to these benefits, setting boundaries and saying no can help individuals develop a stronger sense of self-awareness and self-respect. When individuals are aware of their own needs, values, and priorities, they are better able to honour and respect themselves. This can support the development of self-worth, self-confidence, self-trust, and self-reliance. Additionally, by respecting their own limits and using the word "no" when necessary, individuals demonstrate to themselves and others that they prioritize their own needs and well-being.

Despite the numerous benefits of setting boundaries and saying no, it can be challenging to put these actions into practice. Many individuals may struggle with feelings of guilt, a fear of rejection, or a fear of standing up for their own needs and ideals. However, with clear, assertive communication of one's needs and priorities, as well as consistency in upholding those boundaries, individuals can develop the ability to articulate their demands and limits in a way that feels genuine and respectful.

It can also be helpful for individuals to reflect on any underlying anxieties or beliefs that may be making it difficult to establish boundaries. For example, a fear of conflict or a belief that other people's needs come before one's own may be preventing individuals from asserting their own needs and values. By identifying and addressing these underlying issues, individuals can develop a deeper sense of self-awareness and self-acceptance, which can ultimately lead to greater happiness and fulfillment in all aspects of life.

communication can be a crucial component of setting boundaries and saying no. Assertiveness is the ability to express oneself clearly, honestly, and respectfully while respecting the boundaries of others. It is the balance between passive and aggressive behaviour, and it is an important skill for individuals to develop in order to advocate for their own needs and values.

Learning Assertiveness and clear communication, on the other hand, involves expressing oneself in a way that is easily understood by others. This involves using clear and concise language, active listening, and providing feedback to ensure that the message is received as intended. Clear communication can help prevent misunderstandings, conflicts, and resentment, and it is essential for effective boundary-setting and saying no.

Learning assertiveness and clear communication can be challenging for many people, especially those who have been socialized to prioritize the needs and opinions of others over their own. However, there are several techniques and strategies that can help individuals become more assertive and improve their communication skills.

One effective approach is to practice active listening, which involves giving others your full attention and striving to understand their perspective without passing judgment. This can help individuals build trust and empathy with others, which can lead to more effective communication and stronger relationships.

Another technique is to use "I" statements when expressing oneself. This involves taking responsibility for one's own feelings and opinions rather than placing blame on others. For example, instead of saying "You always interrupt me," one could say "I feel frustrated when I am interrupted."

It is also important to be specific and clear when communicating boundaries or saying no. This may involve setting clear expectations, using direct language, and providing reasons for one's decisions. For example, instead of saying "I can't help you," one could say "I am unable to help you with this task because I have other commitments at the moment."

In addition to these strategies, it is important to practice self-care and self-compassion when learning to set boundaries and say no. This may involve taking time for oneself, setting realistic goals, and recognizing and accepting one's own limitations. It may also involve seeking support from trusted friends, family members, or mental health professionals.

Ultimately, learning to set boundaries and say no is a process that requires practice, patience, and self-awareness. By developing assertiveness and clear communication skills, individuals can advocate for their own needs and values, build stronger relationships, and ultimately lead more fulfilling and authentic lives.

## Developing Self Compassion and Self-Acceptance.

Developing self-authenticity involves a process of steps that include self-compassion and self-acceptance. Being genuine to oneself, being honest with oneself, and having a solid sense of self are all examples of self-authenticity.

It is the cornerstone of self-improvement, personal development, and a happy existence. But cultivating self-authenticity is a challenging task. It necessitates a significant amount of introspection, self-awareness, and self-acceptance. We'll talk about how learning self-compassion and self-acceptance can make us feel more genuine and truer to ourselves in this section.

## What is self-compassion?

The act of being kind to ourselves and treating ourselves as we would a good friend. Sounds easy, right? But let's be real, most of us are harder on ourselves than we are on anyone else. It's like we have this mean inner voice that never shuts up and is always ready to criticize us at any given opportunity.

But what if we could silence that inner voice and replace it with one that is gentle, understanding, and compassionate? That's what self-compassion is all about. It's the practice of treating ourselves with the same kindness and understanding that we would show to someone we care about.

Now, some people might confuse self-compassion with self-pity or self-indulgence. But that's not what it's about at all. Self-compassion is about acknowledging our struggles and difficulties in a kind and understanding way, without getting caught up in a spiral of negativity or self-blame.

Think about it like this: if a friend came to you and told you they were going through a tough time, what would you say to them? You'd probably offer them words of encouragement, support, and understanding, right? You wouldn't tell them to just suck it up and get over it. So why do we treat ourselves any differently?

The truth is, we all face challenges and difficulties in life. It's a natural part of the human experience. But instead of beating ourselves up over our mistakes or shortcomings, we can learn to treat ourselves with the same compassion and kindness that we would show to others.

Self-compassion is not about being perfect or never making mistakes. It's about accepting our imperfections and treating ourselves with kindness and understanding, even when things don't go as planned. It's about recognizing that we are human and that we all make mistakes, but that doesn't mean we are any less worthy of love and compassion.

So, how can we practice self-compassion in our daily lives? Here are a few tips:

1. Practice mindfulness: Mindfulness is the practice of being present and aware of our thoughts and feelings without judgment. By being mindful of our thoughts and feelings, we can recognize when we are being hard on ourselves and learn to replace those negative thoughts with kinder, more compassionate ones.
2. Treat yourself like you would a good friend: When you're going through a tough time, imagine what you would say to a good friend in the same situation. Then, turn those words of kindness and support inward and offer them to yourself.
3. Practice self-care: Taking care of ourselves physically, mentally, and emotionally is a key component of self-compassion. Make time for activities that bring you joy and relaxation and prioritize your well-being.

4. Challenge negative self-talk: When you catch yourself being overly critical or self-blaming, challenge those thoughts with more compassionate and understanding ones. Ask yourself, "Would I say this to a friend?" If the answer is no, then it's time to reframe your thinking.

Remember, self-compassion is not a one-time thing. It's a practice that takes time and effort to cultivate. But with practice, we can learn to treat ourselves with the same kindness and compassion that we show to others and live a happier and more fulfilling life. So go ahead, be kind to yourself.

**What is self-acceptance?**

Ah, self-acceptance, that elusive state of being that seems so simple but can be oh-so-difficult to achieve. It's the act of looking at oneself in the mirror and saying, "Hey, you're pretty great just the way you are!" without any hint of sarcasm or doubt. It's the practice of embracing our flaws, quirks, and imperfections instead of constantly criticizing them.

But let's be real, folks. Self-acceptance is a tricky beast. We live in a world that bombards us with messages that we're not good enough, not pretty enough, not smart enough, not rich enough...the list goes on and on. We're constantly comparing ourselves to others, and in doing so, we forget that we're all unique individuals with our own strengths and weaknesses.

So, what is self-acceptance, really? It's about recognizing and accepting ourselves for who we are, with all of our flaws, limits, and shortcomings. It's not about settling for mediocrity or complacency, but rather embracing the process of self-improvement and personal growth. It's about understanding that we're all works in progress, and that's okay.

Self-acceptance isn't always easy, but it's crucial for our mental health and well-being. When we don't accept ourselves, we're constantly in a state of self-criticism and self-doubt. We're never satisfied with ourselves or our lives, and we're always striving for some unattainable ideal of perfection.

On the other hand, when we practice self-acceptance, we're able to acknowledge our strengths and weaknesses without judgment. We're able to celebrate our successes and learn from our failures. We're able to cultivate a sense of self-worth and self-love that allows us to navigate life's ups and downs with greater ease and resilience.

So, how can we practice self-acceptance in our daily lives? Here are a few tips:

1. Embrace your uniqueness: We're all different, and that's what makes us special. Instead of comparing yourself to others, celebrate your individuality and embrace your quirks and flaws.
2. Challenge negative self-talk: We all have that little voice in our head that tells us we're not good enough. When that voice starts speaking up, challenge it with positive affirmations and reminders of your strengths and accomplishments.
3. Practice self-care: Taking care of yourself physically, mentally, and emotionally is crucial for self-acceptance. Make time for activities that nourish your body and soul, like exercise, meditation, or spending time in nature.
4. Surround yourself with positivity: Surrounding yourself with people who love and support you is key for self-acceptance. Seek out friends and family who uplift you and encourage you to be your best self.
5. Forgive yourself: We all make mistakes, and that's okay. Instead of beating yourself up over past failures, practice self-compassion and forgiveness. Remember that mistakes are opportunities for growth and learning.

6.  Keep a gratitude journal: Focusing on the positive things in your life can help you cultivate a sense of gratitude and appreciation for yourself and your journey. Take time each day to write down things you're grateful for, no matter how small.

Self-acceptance is a journey, not a destination. It's something we must practice every day, in every moment, in order to truly embrace ourselves and our lives. It's not always easy, but it's worth it. When we accept ourselves, we create space for joy, fulfillment, and authentic living. So go ahead, embrace your quirks, celebrate your strengths, and love yourself for who you are. You deserve it!

**Increasing self-acceptance and self-compassion.**

It takes work to cultivate self-compassion and self-acceptance. It calls for a great deal of introspection, self-knowledge, and self-love. Here are some techniques for increasing self-acceptance and self-compassion:

Practice mindfulness: Being mindful is the act of being fully present in the here and now without distraction or judgment. It entails being aware of one's thoughts, feelings, and physical sensations without attempting to alter or regulate them. Self-awareness is a crucial component of growing self-compassion and self-acceptance, and mindfulness aids in the cultivation of self-awareness.

Self-care is the act of looking after one's physical, emotional, and mental well-being. It entails taking actions that advance one's happiness and wellbeing. Self-care might involve exercise, proper nutrition, getting adequate sleep, spending time with beloved ones, pursuing hobbies, and indulging in relaxation practices like as meditation or yoga.

Treat yourself with the same consideration, kindness, and understanding that you would extend to a close friend. This is what it means to be kind to oneself. It entails communicating to oneself in a kind and encouraging way rather than negatively or self-critically.

Cultivate gratitude: Being grateful and appreciative for the wonderful things in one's life is the act of being grateful. Instead of focussing on the negative, it entails putting more of an emphasis on the positive elements of one's life. In order to build self-compassion and self-acceptance, it is crucial to establish a positive mindset and a sense of self-worth.

**How self-acceptance and self-compassion impact one's sense of self.**

Ah, self-acceptance and self-compassion, two peas in a pod when it comes to self-authenticity. Let's break down how they impact one's sense of self:

Self-Awareness: It's like being your own Sherlock Holmes, but instead of solving crimes, you're uncovering your true self. Practicing self-compassion and self-acceptance can aid in developing self-awareness. When we are more in tune with our thoughts, emotions, and values, we are better equipped to understand and accept ourselves. It's like the light bulb turning on in your head, "Oh, so that's why I always feel this way when this happens!" Self-awareness can help us avoid getting caught up in negative emotions like shame or self-doubt. It's like having a superpower that allows you to respond more positively to difficult situations.

Authenticity: Authenticity is like being a unicorn in a world of horses, you stand out because you're unique and true to yourself. When we practice self-compassion, we are more likely to stay true to our values and beliefs, rather than trying to fit in with what others think we should be. It's like having a compass that always points to "true north" or in this case, true self. When we practice self-acceptance, we embrace all aspects of ourselves, the good, the bad, and the ugly. We stop hiding or denying our characteristics and instead learn to love and accept them. It's like finally coming out of the closet, but instead of being gay, you're just being yourself.

Self-confidence: Is the holy grail of self-authenticity. When we practice self-compassion and self-acceptance, we are more likely to feel confident in ourselves and our abilities. We stop comparing ourselves to others and instead focus on our own growth and development. It's like being a turtle that retreats into its shell for protection, but instead of fear, it's a shield of self-confidence. When we accept ourselves as we are, flaws and all, we are more likely to feel a sense of achievement and fulfillment in our lives. It's like a pat on the back, but from yourself.

In conclusion, self-compassion and self-acceptance are key components of self-authenticity. They can help us develop self-awareness, authenticity, and self-confidence. It's like having a secret recipe for a happy and fulfilled life. So, let's be kind and compassionate to ourselves, accept ourselves as we are, and embrace our uniqueness. After all, we're all just trying to navigate this crazy thing called life, so why not do it authentically?

**Self-Compassion and Self-Acceptance Training Techniques.**

Practice mindfulness: Being fully present and conscious of one's thoughts, feelings, and sensations in the present moment while letting go of judgment is the practice of mindfulness. It may be an effective strategy for fostering self-acceptance and compassion. Simple mindfulness exercises like mindful breathing, body scans, and mindful walking are good places to start. These techniques aid people in developing a more accepting and sympathetic view of themselves as well as a greater awareness of their inner sensations.

Practice Self-Care: Growing in self-compassion and self-acceptance requires taking care of oneself Prioritizing self-care activities that support your physical, emotional, and mental health is crucial.

Regular exercise, a balanced diet, proper sleep hygiene, stress management strategies, and enjoyable hobbies are a great place to start making authentic choices. Self-care demonstrates kindness and compassion toward oneself, which can foster greater self-acceptance.

Practice Self-Kindness: Self-kindness refers to treating oneself with the same compassion and kindness as one would a close friend. It entails accepting one's difficulties and errors while also providing encouragement, solace, and understanding to oneself.

This may entail using affirmations, practicing positive self-talk, or composing a letter of self-compassion. People become more accepting and compassionate of themselves when they treat themselves with kindness.

Cultivate gratitude: Being grateful is the act of concentrating on the good things in life rather than dwelling on the bad. It may be an effective strategy for fostering self-acceptance and compassion. One can begin by keeping a thankfulness diary and listing three items each day for which they are thankful. This routine can assist people in adopting a more welcoming and upbeat attitude toward themselves and their lives.

Get Support: One of the most crucial steps in acquiring self-compassion and self-acceptance is seeking support from close friends, family members, or a mental health professional.

Those who talk to someone about their problems, anxieties, and uncertainties often feel more understood, validated, and supported. Also, it can assist people in developing fresh viewpoints and coping mechanisms.

Conclusively, Self-authenticity can be developed via the cultivation of self-compassion and self-acceptance. Individuals can develop these crucial qualities by engaging in self-care, compassion to oneself, gratitude, and mindfulness practices.

People can have more fulfilling lives as they grow in their self-awareness, emotional control, authenticity, and self-confidence. It's crucial to keep in mind that growing in self-compassion and acceptance is a process that takes time, effort, and persistence. Yet, the benefits outweigh the work since they can result in a happier, healthier, and more genuine life.

## Celebrating Individuality and Diversity

The idea of celebrating diversity and individuality has been increasingly important in recent years. It is about accepting and valuing the variations that occur among people in terms of their race, ethnicity, culture, religion, gender, sexual orientation, and many other facets of their identity.

Given the increased diversity of individuals and viewpoints brought about by globalization and multiculturalism in today's globe, this idea has gained relevance.

Because it enables us to comprehend and value the distinctive experiences and viewpoints that each person brings to the table, celebrating individuality and variety is crucial. As a result, we can develop into more true reflections of who we are.

It's crucial to first establish what is meant by authenticity in order to comprehend how valuing uniqueness and diversity can help us become more authentic.

Being real and honest in one's expression of one's values, beliefs, and desires is referred to as authenticity. Being able to present as one's actual self in all spheres of life, including the workplace, intimate partnerships, and social settings, is what it means to be authentic.

By enabling us to explore and appreciate many facets of our identities, celebrating individuality and variety can aid us in becoming more authentic. For instance, if our society places a higher value on some traits than others, we could experience pressure to live up to these norms in order to fit in and be accepted.

Yet, honouring individuality and diversity can help us recognize that there are many various ways of being in the world, and that there is no one "correct" way to be. This can give us the confidence to express these aspects of ourselves more fully and to accept those aspects of ourselves that we may have previously felt ashamed or embarrassed about.

By encouraging a sense of connection and belonging, honouring individuality and diversity can also assist us in being more real. When we are surrounded by people who are unlike us, we are compelled to face our prejudices and presumptions and broaden our horizons.

This can increase our empathy and compassion for other people as well as make us feel more a part of the community. Since we know that we are welcomed and cherished for who we are, when we feel like we belong somewhere, we are more likely to feel at ease expressing ourselves and being our actual selves.

Unfortunately, there are many difficulties that can appear along the route, making it not always simple to celebrate uniqueness and diversity. For instance, some individuals may view diversity as a threat and may react unfavourably to others who are different from them. Others can find it unsettling to consider examining aspects of their identities that go against societal expectations or conventions. Also, to celebrate individuality and diversity, we must be receptive to criticism and constructive criticism as well as open to learning from those with various ideas and life experiences.

Despite these obstacles, it's crucial to keep celebrating variety and individuality because doing so can have a number of advantages for both people and society as a whole. Celebrating diversity and originality can make people more genuine, sympathetic, and compassionate toward others.

Also, it can give them the confidence to express themselves more fully and make them feel more a part of the community. Celebrate diversity and originality to build a more just and equal society where everyone is cherished and respected for who they are.

# Chapter Eight

## NAVIGATING PROFESSIONAL LIFE

Let's face it, navigating the professional world can be a bit like walking on a tightrope while juggling flaming bowling pins. It requires balance, coordination, and a touch of humour to keep from going up in flames. But fear not, dear reader, for with a few tips and tricks, you too can master the art of maintaining authenticity in the workplace.

First and foremost, it's important to recognize the value of self-authenticity. Being true to oneself and expressing oneself in a way that aligns with our core principles and objectives can lead to greater satisfaction and fulfillment in our careers. Plus, it's much easier to remember which version of ourselves we presented to which colleague when we're just being ourselves.

But how does one stay authentic when faced with the pressure to conform to workplace norms and expectations? Well, for starters, it's important to remember that conformity does not equal success. While it may be tempting to blend in with the crowd and go with the flow, it's often those who think outside the box and challenge the status quo that make the biggest impact.

Another way to cultivate authenticity in the workplace is to find common ground with colleagues who share similar values and interests. Forming authentic connections with co-workers not only creates a more positive work environment, but it also allows us to be ourselves without fear of judgment or rejection.

And let's not forget about the power of humour in navigating professional life. A well-placed joke or witty comment can help break down barriers and ease tensions in the workplace. Plus, who doesn't love a colleague who can bring a little levity to the daily grind?

Of course, maintaining authenticity in the workplace isn't always easy. There may be times when we have to make compromises or bite our tongues in order to maintain professional relationships. But as long as we stay true to our core values and beliefs, we can navigate the professional world with confidence and authenticity.

Navigating one's professional life is no small feat, but it's important to remember that we have the power to cultivate authenticity and stay true to ourselves in the process. By valuing our own self-authenticity, challenging workplace norms, forming genuine connections with colleagues, and injecting a little humour into our daily routines, we can navigate the tightrope of professional life with grace and style. So go forth, dear reader, and be your authentic, charming, witty, and intelligent self in all your professional endeavours!

## Determine Your Values and Goals

It's important to take the time to determine your values and goals. These guiding principles will help you stay true to yourself and make decisions that align with your true nature.

Values are the guiding ideas that determine how we conduct our lives. They represent what we believe in and what we stand for. Purpose, on the other hand, is the reason behind what we do. It's what gives us a sense of direction and meaning in life.

By understanding your personal values and purpose, you can link them with the mission and vision of your company. This alignment can help you feel more fulfilled in your work and give you a greater sense of purpose. It also allows you to be true to yourself while still meeting the standards set by your superiors and co-workers.

Of course, discovering your values and purpose is easier said than done. It requires a bit of self-reflection and introspection. Start by asking yourself some key questions: What do I stand for? What drives me? What do I want to achieve in life?

Once you have a clear understanding of your values and purpose, it's important to communicate them to your colleagues and superiors. Let them know what's important to you and how it aligns with the goals of the company. This not only helps you stay true to yourself, but it also helps create a positive work environment based on shared values and goals.

**Be Clear About Your Wants and Limitations.**

It's a delicate dance that many of us struggle with in the workplace. But the truth is, being clear about your wants and limitations is essential for cultivating self-authenticity and maintaining a healthy work-life balance.

So, how can you communicate your needs and boundaries effectively? Well, it starts with being honest with yourself about what you're comfortable with and what you're not. This may involve setting reasonable expectations for yourself and others and asking for help when necessary.

Once you have a clear understanding of your wants and limitations, it's important to communicate them to your co-workers and superiors. This can be done in a respectful and professional manner, while still maintaining your authenticity. Remember, it's okay to say "no" when something doesn't align with your values or goals.

By being clear about your needs and boundaries, you can build healthy relationships with your colleagues and superiors. This not only fosters a positive work environment, but it also helps reduce burnout and promotes overall well-being.

Of course, setting boundaries is easier said than done. It can be uncomfortable and even scary to assert oneself in the workplace. But the benefits of doing so are well worth it. By staying true to yourself and communicating your needs and limitations effectively, you can create a work environment that aligns with your values and promotes your overall well-being.

Being clear about your wants and limitations is essential for cultivating self-authenticity in the workplace. By setting reasonable expectations for yourself and others, communicating your needs and boundaries effectively, and asking for help, when necessary, you can build healthy relationships with your colleagues and superiors and promote a positive work-life balance. So go ahead and assert yourself with confidence, dear reader. Your authentic self will thank you for it.

**Be Sincere in All of Your Encounters.**

Being sincere and truthful in one's communication with others is a requirement for authenticity in interactions. It is expressing one's thoughts and feelings without fear of judgment or rejection. Authenticity in communication can help people establish rapport and trust with subordinates and superiors, which can foster cooperation and teamwork.

Being real in encounters can also help individuals create their personal brand and reputation. Individuals can differentiate themselves in the workplace and appreciated for their contributions by expressing their distinctive viewpoints and ideas.

**Accept Your Strengths and Weaknesses**

the age-old adage of "know thyself." It's a phrase that rings true in all aspects of life, including the workplace. Accepting your strengths and weaknesses is a crucial step towards cultivating self-authenticity and achieving personal and professional success.

So, what does it mean to accept your strengths and weaknesses? It means acknowledging your unique talents and abilities while also recognizing areas where you can improve. It's about having confidence in your skills and being open to learning and growth.

By accepting your strengths, you can identify your niche in the workplace and contribute to the success of your team. You can also build confidence in your abilities and work towards achieving your personal and professional goals.

At the same time, accepting your weaknesses can be a powerful motivator for growth and development. It encourages a growth mentality, where you're open to learning new skills and improving yourself. It's important to remember that everyone has weaknesses, and it's okay to ask for help or seek out resources to overcome them.

Of course, accepting your strengths and weaknesses isn't always easy. It can be tempting to focus solely on our strengths and ignore areas where we may need improvement. But the truth is, acknowledging and addressing our weaknesses can be the key to unlocking our full potential and achieving success in the workplace.

Accepting your strengths and weaknesses is essential for cultivating self-authenticity and achieving personal and professional success. By having confidence in your skills, identifying your niche in the workplace, and being open to learning and growth, you can achieve great things. So embrace your strengths and weaknesses with open arms, dear reader. Your authentic self will thank you for it.

### Look for Possibilities for Advancement and Growth.

The pursuit of growth and advancement. It's a common goal for many of us in the workplace, and for good reason. Seeking out opportunities for development is a key aspect of cultivating self-authenticity and achieving personal and professional success.

So, what does it mean to look for possibilities for advancement and growth? It means being proactive in seeking out new challenges, learning opportunities, and ways to expand your skills and expertise. This could involve attending training sessions, taking on new responsibilities, or even going back to school.

By looking for opportunities for growth and development, you can increase your value to your employer and become more useful in your role. It also helps to keep you engaged and motivated in your work, as you're constantly learning and challenging yourself.

Of course, seeking out growth and advancement isn't always easy. It may involve stepping out of your comfort zone and taking on new challenges. But the benefits of doing so are well worth it. By expanding your skills and expertise, you can unlock new opportunities for personal and professional success.

In conclusion, looking for possibilities for advancement and growth is essential for cultivating self-authenticity in the workplace. By seeking out new challenges and learning opportunities, you can increase your value to your employer, stay engaged in your work, and achieve personal and professional success. So go forth, dear reader, and pursue your growth and advancement with gusto. Your authentic self will thank you for it.

### Finding and Pursuing Meaningful Work.

Finding and pursuing meaningful job can have a significant impact on our self-authenticity today where we spend a lot of time at work. When our inner selves and the roles we perform in our daily lives are in harmony, this drives up your self-authenticity. We are more likely to have a sense of fulfilment, contentment, and purpose when we are working on worthwhile projects, which can improve our general wellbeing.

Finding and pursuing occupations that fit our interests, values, and strengths is part of the search for meaningful work. It necessitates a thorough comprehension of who we are and what motivates us. We are more likely to be our true selves at work when we are doing something that is meaningful to us. Increased creativity and invention, improved connections with co-workers, and greater job happiness can all result from this.

We can improve our feeling of self by pursuing meaningful job, which is one of the main advantages. We become more conscious of who we are and what we stand for when we work on projects that are in line with our values and passions. This self-awareness can be applied to various facets of our existence, such as our hobbies and interpersonal interactions. As we progress toward our objectives, we grow more self-assured in our skills and prepared to take chances.

Work that is relevant to us can also boost our motivation and involvement. We are more likely to go above and beyond what is required of us when we are passionate about our profession. If we put more effort into our work, we are more likely to feel a sense of ownership over it. Better performance and improved levels of productivity may result from this elevated engagement.

Working on meaningful projects can also give us a sense of direction. We are more likely to feel that we are making a significant contribution to society when we work on projects that are in line with our values and interests. This may result in a sense of contentment and happiness that can be challenging to get from other sources.

Finding and pursuing meaningful work, however, can be difficult. It necessitates a thorough grasp of who we are and what we hope to achieve in our jobs.

The following points can aid us to achieve this:

- Consider your values and passions: Give yourself some time to consider your values and areas of interest. Consider the principles that guide you and the pursuits that make you the happiest. You can determine the kinds of work that would be most significant to you with the aid of this reflection.

- Determine your strengths by taking into account the abilities and skills you have. Consider the jobs and pursuits that you are naturally good at. This might assist you in determining the kinds of jobs that would enable you to make use of your skills and abilities.

- Once your values, interests, and strengths have been determined, look into occupations that fit these characteristics. Search for professions that would enable you to carry out work that is important to you.

- Speak to people in the fields that interest you by networking. Get in touch with specialists for informational interviews by attending networking events. This can give you a better idea of the job's requirements and whether you'd be a suitable fit for it.

- If you are unclear of the kind of work that might be important to you, try taking a course or volunteering in an area that interests you. This can enable you to obtain experience in the field and decide if it's something you want to pursue further.

**Creating a Work-Life balance that aligns with personal values.**

The elusive work-life balance. It's something that many of us strive for, but few of us achieve. But with a little effort and focus, it is possible to create a work-life balance that aligns with our personal values and allows us to lead a more fulfilling life.

The first step in achieving a work-life balance that aligns with our personal values is to understand what those values are. This may involve some introspection and reflection, but it's crucial to establish what's most important to us in life.

Once we have a clear understanding of our personal values, we can assess how our current work-life balance fits with those values. Are we giving enough time to the things that matter most to us, or are we consumed by work and neglecting other areas of our lives?

Setting clear boundaries between work and personal time is a key aspect of achieving a work-life balance that aligns with our personal values. This may involve creating a schedule for our professional and personal time and being strict about sticking to it. Saying no to requests that don't align with our values is also an important skill to develop.

But achieving a work-life balance that aligns with our personal values goes beyond just setting boundaries and saying no. It's also about finding ways to incorporate our personal values into our work and professional lives. For example, if we value creativity, we can look for ways to incorporate it into our work by brainstorming new ideas or coming up with innovative solutions to problems. If we value collaboration, we can seek out opportunities to work closely with our colleagues.

In addition to infusing our personal values into our work, it's important to find ways to live out those values outside of work as well. This may involve pursuing a new hobby or passion project that aligns with our values and gives us a sense of fulfillment outside of our professional lives.

It's important to remember that achieving a work-life balance that aligns with our personal values is an ongoing process. It takes constant effort and focus, and it's not something that can be accomplished overnight. But by giving priority to our personal values and making deliberate decisions about how we spend our time, we can create a work-life balance that allows us to pursue our goals and lead a more fulfilling life.

Creating a work-life balance that aligns with our personal values is essential for cultivating self-authenticity and achieving personal and professional success. By understanding our personal values, setting clear boundaries, and infusing our values into our work and personal lives, we can create a more fulfilling and balanced life. So go forth, dear reader, and create a work-life balance that aligns with your values and brings you happiness and fulfillment. Your authentic self will thank you for it

**Negotiating Workplace dynamic and politics**

Navigating workplace dynamics and politics can be a daunting task, but it's a necessary one if you want to advance your career and achieve professional success. While it's always best to take the high road and behave honourably, there are times when you may need to be strategic in your approach.

Here are some tips for negotiating workplace dynamics and politics:

1.  Build relationships: Building relationships with your colleagues and superiors is key to navigating workplace politics. Take the time to get to know people and show an interest in their work and ideas. This can help you build trust and credibility, which can be invaluable when it comes to navigating office politics.

2.  Keep your emotions in check: Workplace politics can be emotional, but it's important to keep your emotions in check. Avoid getting defensive or confrontational, and instead, stay calm and professional. This can help you maintain control of the situation and avoid making any missteps that could damage your reputation.

3.  Be proactive: It's always better to be proactive than reactive when it comes to workplace politics. Keep an eye out for potential issues or conflicts and take steps

to address them before they escalate. This can help you stay ahead of the game and maintain a positive reputation.

4. Stay true to your values: It's important to stay true to your values and principles, even in the face of workplace politics. Don't compromise your integrity or ethical standards in order to get ahead. Instead, find ways to advance your career while staying true to who you are and what you believe in.

5. Seek guidance: If you're unsure how to navigate a particular workplace dynamic or political situation, seek guidance from a mentor or trusted colleague. They may be able to offer insights and advice that can help you navigate the situation more effectively.

Negotiating workplace dynamics and politics can be challenging, but it's a necessary part of advancing your career and achieving professional success. By building relationships, keeping your emotions in check, being proactive, staying true to your values, and seeking guidance when needed, you can navigate workplace politics with confidence and integrity.

## Understanding the politics and dynamics at work

Understanding the politics and dynamics at work can be challenging, but it's an essential skill if you want to advance in your career. Here are some tips for gaining a better understanding of the office politics and dynamics:

1. Pay attention to actions and words: People may say one thing but do another, so it's important to pay attention to both actions and words. Observe how people behave and interact with others and consider whether their actions match up with what they say.

2. Listen and observe: Listen to conversations and watch how people interact with each other. Pay attention to body language and voice tone, as these can provide important clues about the underlying dynamics at play.

3. Keep an open mind: Don't be too quick to judge or draw conclusions based on first impressions or rumours. It's important to keep an open mind and consider different perspectives.

4. Get input from co-workers: Your colleagues may be able to provide valuable insights into the dynamics at work. Don't be afraid to ask for their input or advice.

5. Ask questions: If you're unsure about something, don't be afraid to ask questions. Understanding the goals and potential risks of a situation can help you make informed decisions and navigate challenging circumstances with confidence.

In conclusion, understanding office politics and dynamics is an important skill for anyone looking to advance in their career. By paying attention to actions and words, listening, and observing, keeping an open mind, getting input from co-workers, and asking questions, you can gain a better understanding of the underlying dynamics at play and navigate the workplace more effectively.

**Advice on How to Effectively Negotiate Office Politics.**

Although dealing with workplace politics can be stressful, doing so successfully is essential for your professional development and general well-being. Here are some pointers to assist you in navigating any office politics.

- Be careful with your language and your interactions with employees, especially those in positions of authority. Even when discussions get hot, maintain your composure, pay close attention as you listen, and always be polite and open-minded. Even if you don't agree with the other person's viewpoint, demonstrate that you comprehend it.

- Second, develop connections with those who are influential within the organization. It's more probable that your ideas will be taken seriously the more individuals who know and trust you there are! Speak to co-workers about subjects other than work in order to foster good relationships between peers.

- Next, exercise diplomacy while interacting with challenging situations or people. If someone criticizes or challenges something you did, step back, give it some thought, and then answer respectfully rather than angrily. Instead of focusing on winning a debate, try to comprehend; it will be more effective in the long run.

- Finally, keep a positive attitude and concentrate on finding answers as opposed to pointing the finger at or criticizing others. Keep in mind that everyone is striving for the same thing: the success of the company. By concentrating on how to get there, everyone will gain in the long run.

### How to Be Assertive Without Being Rude.

How can you be assertive without becoming hostile? The key to navigating workplace relationships and politics is learning how to be aggressive and set boundaries. The key is to practice "assertive communication," which entails strongly and respectfully expressing your thoughts.

*You can be assertive by using the following advice:*

- Use first-person narration. Instead of blaming or making excuses for others, talk in the first person to own your thoughts and feelings.

- Employ a "I statement" to communicate your feelings without criticizing or attacking anyone else. Saying "I feel like my ideas are not being heard," as opposed to "You never listen to my ideas" or "Nobody listens to me around here," is an excellent example.

- Recognize when it's appropriate to have a frank discussion with your manager or co-workers about establishing boundaries and expectations at work. Decide in advance what you want the conversation to accomplish so that you are prepared.

- To ensure that everyone has been heard, appreciated, and understood, actively listen by posing questions and repeating back what you hear from others.

- Maintaining good body language, such as smiling, maintaining eye contact, leaning forward, nodding, and providing constructive criticism, when necessary, demonstrates your interest in and involvement in the conversation.

- You can masterfully negotiate workplace dynamics and politics by using the advice in this article on effective communication, all while avoiding being confrontational or rude to other participants.

**Understanding Typical Power Plays at Work.**

Power plays at work are frequently covert and challenging to spot. It's crucial to understand what they are and how to defend yourself against them. Here are a few typical power plays to watch out for:

- Giving Others Credit for Their Work

Taking credit for other people's labour in order to elevate their own status at work is one of the most prevalent power plays. The ability to spot this conduct and call it out when you see it is crucial. Also, it's a good idea to keep track of your own work so that, in the event that someone tries to take credit for it, you can demonstrate your ownership of it.

- Suppressing Co-workers

When someone tries to quiet their colleagues by downplaying their thoughts or opinions, that is another example of a power play. This is frequently done to exert control over events or to ensure that their opinions are heard over everyone else's. It's crucial to defend your co-workers and make sure their views are heard if you see this happening.

- Playing with the System

Another typical strategy is to manipulate the system itself, changing due dates, policies, and procedures to your advantage. This is a sort of power play that ought to be avoided at all costs; nobody ever wants to take advantage of someone else's effort or success in order to further their own interests.

Knowing what to look for can help you stay out of power plays and workplace politics in the first place. Being aware of them and being able to spot them when they happen is the best defence against them.

**How to Deal with Passive Aggressive Co-workers.**

Dealing with passive-aggressive co-workers can be challenging, but it's important to handle the situation professionally and assertively. Here are some tips for handling passive-aggressive behaviour in the workplace:

1. Keep your cool: When dealing with a passive-aggressive co-worker, it's important to remain calm and composed. Avoid reacting emotionally or engaging in an argument. Instead, speak firmly but politely and maintain a neutral tone.
2. Make the conversation two-way: Encourage your co-worker to communicate openly and express their thoughts and feelings. This can help them feel respected and included and may lead to a mutually agreeable solution.

3. Don't take it personally: Remember that a co-worker' passive-aggressive behaviour is likely not about you personally. Try not to take it too personally and remain focused on finding a solution to the issue at hand.

4. Remain professional: No matter how difficult the situation may be, it's important to maintain professionalism and composure. Avoid getting emotional or engaging in unprofessional behaviour.

5. Maintain your concentration: Stay focused on the task at hand and don't let your emotions get the best of you. Take a step back and consider the situation logically before responding or reacting.

6. Communicate politely: Always communicate in a respectful and professional manner, even if your co-worker is not doing the same. Avoid getting into a back-and-forth argument and stay focused on finding a solution to the issue.

In conclusion, dealing with passive-aggressive co-workers can be challenging, but it's important to handle the situation assertively and professionally. By keeping your cool, making the conversation two-way, not taking it personally, remaining professional, maintaining your concentration, and communicating politely, you can effectively navigate the situation and maintain good working relationships with your co-workers.

## Balancing Self Authenticity and Office Politics

Being loyal to oneself and expressing one's personality are becoming increasingly important today. This emphasis on self-authenticity is crucial because it enables people to live lives that are true to their ideals and convictions.

Self-authenticity can be challenging to manage in the workplace while still managing office politics. The term "office politics" describes the methods and techniques people employ to advance their status and influence at work.

This section will discuss the value of striking a balance between self-authenticity and office politics and offer advice for surviving this treacherous environment.

## Why Self-Authenticity Matters

Self-authenticity is necessary for happiness and contentment on a personal level. Those who are true to themselves can lead lives that are consistent with their values and convictions. Increased happiness, job satisfaction, and general wellbeing can result from this.

Self-authenticity can also be a strong benefit in the workplace. Genuine people are frequently regarded as trustworthy and dependable, which can promote respect and appreciation from subordinates and superiors. Also, as they are unrestricted by cultural standards and expectations, people who are true to themselves frequently exhibit greater creativity and innovation.

## How Important Are Office Politics.

Self-authenticity is crucial, but it's not the only thing that makes people successful at work. Most businesses have office politics, and people who can successfully negotiate these politics frequently have better career success.

Office politics can take many different shapes, from creating connections with powerful people to using diplomatic and negotiating strategies. These strategies are employed to increase one's position of authority and access to resources at work.

Office politics experts can create meaningful connections and networks that can result in more employment possibilities and promotions. These people can also affect choices and results in the workplace, which can improve job satisfaction and a feeling of accomplishment.

## Managing Office Politics and Self-Authenticity.

It can be difficult for people to strike a balance between their demand for self-authenticity and their need to successfully negotiate office politics. Although these two elements may appear to be in opposition to one another, there are strategies to successfully balance them.

- Be Clear About Your Priorities and Principles

Being certain of your principles and priorities is the first step in striking a balance between self-authenticity and office politics. Making decisions that are in line with your beliefs and objectives will be easier if you are aware of what is most important to you.

Asking yourself how this circumstance fits with your values and priorities can help you when you must negotiate office politics. If the circumstances are not favourable, it might be best to stay away from them or find a strategy to deal with them that is consistent with your moral principles.

- Create Networks and Relationships

Developing networks and relationships is crucial for successfully managing office politics. Yet it's crucial to do so in a true and authentic manner.

Focus on establishing connections with people who share your priorities and values when forming relationships. This will assist you in creating a network of people who are supportive of you and your objectives.

- Use Strategic Communication in Your Work

Office politics require effective communication. To ensure that you are expressing yourself truthfully while still navigating workplace politics successfully, it is crucial to be smart in your communication.

Be concise and straightforward while talking with subordinates and colleagues. Avoid engaging in gossip or badmouthing others because doing so might harm your relationships and reputation.

- Be adaptable.

Being adaptable is a key quality for handling office politics. Being true to yourself is crucial, but it's also critical to be flexible and receptive to fresh perspectives.

Be adaptable in how you approach situations where you must negotiate office politics. Be willing to compromise if it is consistent with your values and priorities while taking into account various viewpoints and ideas.

- Constrain your emotions.

For many people, office politics may be a source of stress and annoyance. When navigating these politics, it's crucial to control your emotions.

Keep your negative emotions, like resentment or rage, at bay. Instead, concentrate on maintaining composure and a cool head while responding to circumstances logically and clearly.

- Seek Assistance.

It can be difficult to navigate office politics, so it's critical to ask for help when you need it. This can be provided through mentors, co-workers, or friends outside the office.

Finding support can help you stay committed to your objectives while offering helpful insight and counsel while dealing with challenging circumstances.

- Continue to be yourself.

Finally, it is important to stay loyal to yourself when negotiating office politics. While it may be tempting to sacrifice your morals or principles to increase your influence or authority, doing so can eventually cause you to feel unhappy and dissatisfied.

Instead, concentrate on figuring out how to negotiate office politics in a way that is consistent with your priorities and values. Although it could take some time and effort, doing this will ultimately result in a more rewarding and meaningful profession.

Self-authenticity and office politics can be difficult to balance. However, you can successfully navigate office politics while remaining true to yourself by being clear on your values and priorities, developing relationships and networks, being strategic in your communication, being flexible, keeping your emotions in check, seeking support, and remaining true to yourself. By doing this, you can advance your job while preserving your fulfilment and well-being on a personal level.

# Chapter Nine

## AUTHENTICITY AND CULTURAL IDENTITY

What does it entail to be who we are? Are all of us the result of our cultural upbringings and society norms? In a society where conformity and compliance are paramount, how can we keep our authenticity?

You undoubtedly ask yourself questions like these on a frequent basis. And that's okay because it shows that you're actively trying to explore your identity and have a deeper understanding of yourself. The idea of self-authenticity has gained popularity recently as more people want for approval from others and a sense of belonging to their group and culture.

In this chapter, we'll examine the value of self-authenticity in contemporary culture, how it relates to identity, and how you might begin your quest for self-authenticity.

**Authenticity and Identity: An Exploration.**

Discovering identity and authenticity may be a scary endeavour. Since our identities are shaped by our environments, families, and cultures, there may be a lot of internal struggles. What characterizes you? What distinguishes true living from merely following social conventions?

Finding balance requires taking the time to comprehend the numerous elements that make up your personality, which is a crucial first step. This entails investigating the ways in which your cultural upbringing has influenced your ideas and values, recognizing the influences of society on how you see yourself, and discovering the reasons behind the values that are significant to you.

Once you have a deeper knowledge of each of these components, you can begin to evaluate which one's support who you truly are, and which ones do not.

Self-reflection and open introspection are the first steps on the path to living a genuine life. You can develop a genuine sense of self-understanding that will guide you on your journey to becoming the best version of yourself by accepting both the good and the bad aspects of your personality.

Ponder on your values and beliefs: Take some time to think about what means most to you and what you believe in. Examine whether there are any conflicts or contradictions between your ideals and your cultural background.

Analyse your past encounters: Consider the ways in which both your experiences and your sense of self have been shaped by your cultural identity. Think about the ways in which your culture has shaped your views, convictions, and actions.

Interact with people from various backgrounds and cultures to broaden your perspective and improve your understanding of other civilizations. This can help you appreciate your own culture while also appreciating and valuing others.

Appreciate our individual differences and be appreciative of the diversity in the world around you by embracing diversity. You may increase your level of cultural knowledge and respect for other people by embracing variety.

Get support: When you investigate your self-authenticity and cultural identity, it may be beneficial to seek support from friends, family, or a therapist. Along the journey, they can provide direction, affirmation, and support.

**Making Sense of Cultural Identity.**

It's crucial to understand that there are numerous components to our cultural identity when we consider where we originate from in terms of our values, beliefs, practices, and traditions. The way that people define their cultural identities might be very different. Our perceptions of ourselves, other people, and our place in the world are shaped by a variety of worldviews, viewpoints, and contexts.

Despite having a sense of belonging to a certain culture, many people struggle with their own sense of self, whether as a result of tensions in their ancestry or shifts in viewpoint as they enter adulthood. Even within the same culture, self-identity can be highly diverse and complex because we are all shaped by our own experiences.

Learning how to uphold one's individuality while embracing influences from different cultures is difficult. The process of creating an authentic cultural identity can be time- and effort-consuming. To accomplish this successfully, you must learn to identify your distinct fundamental beliefs and values and fight to advance them without feeling pressure to fit in or conform to others.

## Cultural influences on self-authenticity

Cultural influences greatly influence how people perceive and communicate their sense of self. The following cultural elements can have an impact on one's sense of self:

- Collectivism vs. Individualism

Two cultural influences that might have a big impact on one's sense of self-authenticity are collectivism and individualism.

A cultural value known as collectivism emphasizes the value of the group over the individual. People tend to define themselves in collectivist cultures in terms of their connections to other people, such as their family, community, or social group. Instead of individuality and rivalry, the focus is on interdependence and cooperation.

On the other side, individualism is a cultural value that places more emphasis on the importance of the person than the group. People tend to identify themselves in terms of their own accomplishments, objectives, and ambitions in individualistic cultures. Instead of collectivism and conformity, the emphasis is on freedom and self-reliance.

Self-authenticity may be significantly impacted by certain cultural beliefs. People may put the needs and expectations of the group ahead of their own interests and objectives in collectivist settings.

A sense of uniformity and a reluctance to exhibit individuality may result from this. On the other side, individuals may put their own interests and aspirations ahead of the needs of the group in individualistic societies, which can result in a feeling of alienation and detachment.

Being loyal to oneself and expressing one's distinct identity, values, and opinions are both components of self-authenticity. Individuals may experience pressure in collectivist cultures to suppress their individuality and adhere to the expectations of the collective, which might impede their capacity to be self-authentic. People in individualistic cultures could experience pressure to live up to success expectations and societal norms, which can impede their capacity to be authentically themselves.

In summary, societies that place more emphasis on collectivism tend to value conformity and interdependence whereas societies that place more emphasis on individualism tend to value self-expression and independence. Those who live in collectivistic cultures could experience greater pressure to fit in and put fitting in above being authentic.

- Power Distance

The degree to which people in a community accept and expect an unequal allocation of power among individuals and organizations is referred to as power distance. There is a higher emphasis on hierarchical connections and authority in communities with a high-power distance, whereas there is a stronger emphasis on equality and individualism in civilizations with a low power distance.

The degree to which people feel true to themselves and behave in ways that are congruent with their own values, beliefs, and preferences can be impacted by power distance.

People may be more willing to follow social norms and expectations in societies with high power distances, even if those expectations go against their own personal values and opinions. This may put pressure on them to hide or suppress parts of who they really are in order to blend in and not stick out. As a result, people who live in high power distance societies could feel less honest about themselves.

On the other hand, people might be freer to express themselves and behave in ways that are compatible with their own personal values and views in societies with minimal power distance.

- Gender Roles

A collection of cultural expectations and standards about how people should behave based on their gender are known as gender roles. The degree to which someone feels genuine and true to their own identity can have an impact on how these roles on a person's self-authenticity.

Different gender roles are expected in different cultures, which can have an impact on one's sense of self. People might feel pressure to fit into gender stereotypes, for instance, in societies that place a high value on traditional gender roles. This can limit people's ability to express who they truly are.

The imposition of strict expectations on people based on their gender is one way that gender roles can have an impact on self-authenticity. Men, for instance, could feel pressure to be tough and unflappable, whereas women might feel pressure to be loving and sentimental. For people who do not meet these stereotypes, these expectations can lead to conflict and a lack of self-authenticity.

Furthermore, gender roles may restrict a person from expressing their true selves. Men, for instance, could find it difficult to show their sensitivity or feelings out of concern that they will be perceived as weak, whereas women might feel restricted from pursuing particular occupations or pastimes because they are not deemed "feminine." These restrictions may impede people from exploring and expressing their true selves to the fullest.

Yet, rejecting conventional gender stereotypes can also be a means for people to stand up for their authenticity. For instance, a non-binary person could decide to display themselves in a way that defies conventional gender norms, which can be an empowering expression of their true selves.

- Religion

People's perceptions of their sense of self can be influenced by their religious views. Those who practice religions that emphasize humility and selflessness, for instance, could see self-expression as a sign of pride and feel under pressure to hide their true selves.

A person's sense of self and authenticity can be significantly shaped by their religious beliefs. The teachings and practices of various religions can have an effect on how people regard themselves and their place in the world.

The ideals and beliefs that religion espouses are one way in which it may have an impact on self-authenticity. For instance, even if it goes against their natural tendencies, someone who is nurtured in a religious culture that values humility may place a larger focus on being humble and self-effacing.

On the other hand, a person may place more importance on self-expression and assertiveness if they were taught in a religious tradition that promotes individualism and personal success.

Religion can also foster a sense of belonging and community, which can play a significant role in the growth of self-authenticity. A person's entire sense of identity and authenticity can be boosted by the support, direction, and feeling of purpose that belonging to a religious group can provide.

But, when religion conflicts with a person's personal values and views, it can also be a source of conflict and dissonance. For instance, a person may find it difficult to reconcile their differences with their sense of self if they have doubts about some of the principles of their religion or disagree with certain features of their religious group.

The effect of religion on one's sense of self-authenticity ultimately varies from person to person and is influenced by a range of personal and cultural variables. While religion can provide people a sense of identity and community, it can also cause conflict and undermine their sense of self.

- Race and ethnicity

Race and ethnicity can significantly affect a person's sense of self and authenticity, as well ae values, beliefs, and experiences.

Racial or ethnic identity plays a significant role in a person's identity, depending on how strongly they identify with their cultural heritage. They may feel a great sense of connection and pride for their cultural group, and they may work hard to preserve or express their cultural identity in many ways.

People with varied ethnic and racial backgrounds could encounter particular cultural pressures and expectations that have an impact on their sense of self-authenticity. Those from marginalized groups, for instance, could experience pressure to fit in with prevailing cultural standards, which might restrict their ability to express their true cultural identities.

Yet, for people who do not have a strong connection to their cultural background or who may feel marginalized or excluded due to their race or ethnicity, a person's sense of self and authenticity may be more challenging.

It's possible that they will feel pressure to conform to cultural norms or expectations that don't necessarily align with their own values or beliefs. This can cause internal conflict or dissonance.

Furthermore, a person's sense of self and authenticity may be further clouded by the junction of their racial and ethnic identity with other aspects of their identity, such as their gender, sexual orientation, or social status. For example, people who identify as being part of a racially or ethnically marginalized group may feel more authentic when they are free to fully express their gender identity or sexual orientation, but they may have more trouble doing so due to cultural norms or discrimination.

In the end, the relationship between self-authenticity and race and ethnicity is nuanced and dependent on an individual's experiences, beliefs, and ideals. People should analyse and reflect on their cultural identity to gain a better understanding of how it could affect their sense of self and authenticity.

- Communication Style

An important cultural component that might influence someone's sense of self-authenticity is communication style. Different communication techniques among cultures may have an impact on how one expresses oneself. For instance, cultures that emphasize direct communication may place a higher importance on honesty and openness than cultures that place a higher value on harmony and preventing disagreement.

People are encouraged to openly and immediately communicate their views and feelings in cultures where direct communication is valued. People may feel more at ease and sincere in their expression as a result of this. On the other hand, people may feel pressured to be less expressive or to speak in a more indirect fashion in societies where indirect communication is encouraged, which can result in sentiments of inauthenticity.

Moreover, communication style can influence how people interpret and react to feedback. People may be more inclined to view criticism as a chance for growth and improvement in settings where receiving direct and critical feedback is encouraged, which can strengthen their sense of self-authenticity. Yet, people may be more prone to see input as a personal attack in environments where indirect or non-confrontational feedback is valued, which might weaken their feeling of self-authenticity.

Ultimately, a person's self-authenticity can be greatly impacted by the cultural element of communication style. People can negotiate cross-cultural communication and express themselves more honestly by being aware of how different communication styles exist across cultures.

- Historical Context

Self-authenticity can be greatly influenced by historical context because culture and history can influence how we understand who we are and how we express ourselves. Values, beliefs, and traditions that are deeply embedded in a society's historical framework can have an impact on how people understand and express who they truly are.

Cultural traditions and historical occurrences can mold a culture's values and beliefs, which can have an impact on self-authenticity. Cultures that have endured oppression or cultural absorption, for instance, might place a higher priority on conformity to prevent continued marginalization.

For instance, historical occurrences like wars, colonization, and social movements can influence how people from various cultural origins perceive and articulate their identities.

Those who have gone through social movements that challenge cultural norms may feel emboldened to express their true selves more openly, in contrast to those who have suffered colonization or assimilation, which may make it difficult for them to restore their cultural identity.

Cultural values and traditions can influence how people perceive their true selves. For instance, individuals may put fitting in with their group above expressing their distinctive personality in countries where collectivism and conformity are strongly valued.

People could feel more at ease expressing themselves in a way that is consistent with their particular values and beliefs in other cultures, on the other hand, that place a higher priority on individualism.

Ultimately, historical context as a cultural component can have a range of effects on self-authenticity, including influencing how people perceive themselves, shaping cultural norms and customs, and changing how they feel comfortable expressing themselves.

- Socialization

How people are socialized within their culture can have an impact on how they feel about themselves. The cultural influence of socialization on a person's sense of self and capacity for honest expression can be profound.

The process by which people pick up and assimilate the rules, values, beliefs, and actions of their society or culture is referred to as socialization. These cultural influences may influence how people see themselves and their place in society, which may have a big impact on how real they may be.

Those who were trained to value social peace, for instance, could find it difficult to express who they truly are if it goes against social expectations.

The absorption of cultural norms and values is one way that socialization can have an impact on self-authenticity. There are standards for how people should act, dress, and interact with others in many different cultures. If people stray from these expectations, these norms and values may put pressure on them to live up to them, which may make it harder for them to express who they truly are.

People could feel pressure to comply to these expectations even if it conflicts with their genuine selves, for instance, if their society places a high importance on compliance and conformity.

Socialization can also affect a person's self-concept, or how they perceive themselves. Even if they do not reflect their true selves, people may adopt features or attributes that are highly valued in a culture into their self-concept. For instance, people may prioritize achievement and material prosperity in their self-concept even though these goals are at odds with their genuine beliefs and values.

- Education

Educational systems can influence cultural values and beliefs, which can have an impact on a person's sense of self. The following are some ways that education may affect one's level of self-authenticity:

Education may promote individuality by giving students chances for self-expression, critical thinking, and creativity. People are more likely to acquire a genuine and accurate sense of self when they are encouraged to express themselves.

Exposing people to a variety of viewpoints: Education can expose people to a range of viewpoints, cultures, and ideas. They may have a deeper awareness of the world and a more complex sense of who they are as a result of this exposure.

Promoting personal development: Education can assist people in acquiring new abilities, information, and experiences that advance their personal development. Individuals may be able to express themselves more honestly and with better self-awareness as a result of this progress.

Establishing social norms: Education can also establish norms for identity and behaviour. For instance, some educational institutions like schools may promote adherence to predetermined social or cultural norms. If their expression does not meet these expectations, this may restrict their ability to be authentic.

- Economic Situation

Self-authenticity, which is the degree to which people feel true to themselves and their ideals, can be greatly impacted by economic circumstances.

Here are some examples of how the state of the economy might affect one's sense of self:

Economic stress: People's feeling of self-authenticity may be impacted when they are having trouble making ends meet or dealing with other financial issues. If they are unable to support themselves or their family, they may feel pressured to compromise their morals in order to increase their income or may experience feelings of guilt or inadequacy.

Social class: A person's sense of identity and self-perception can be greatly influenced by their social class, which in turn can be greatly influenced by their economic condition. The attitudes, beliefs, and lifestyles of people from various economic origins may differ, which may affect how they feel about themselves and how real they are.

Professional identity: A crucial component of self-authenticity, professional identity can be impacted by the economy. For instance, people who are having trouble finding work or who have positions that don't fit with their skills or values may feel unauthentic or unsatisfied with their career path.

Materialism: A person's sense of self and authenticity can be impacted by materialism and consumerism, which are also influenced by the economy. Individuals who place a higher importance on material belongings or riches than other values may experience feelings of emptiness or unfulfillment, which may affect how they view themselves.

As a result, the state of the economy can be a crucial cultural issue that has an array of effects on self-authenticity. In order to make sure they are remaining loyal to themselves and their convictions in the face of economic stress or social class distinctions, it is crucial for people to reflect on their values and priorities.

It's crucial to remember that cultural influences are not deterministic, and people can still decide to express their true selves in the face of societal pressures. To better manage cultural differences and find methods to express our authentic selves within our cultural setting, it can be helpful to understand how culture can shape our sense of self.

### Self-awareness exercises and accepting change.

Being self-aware and accepting of change are crucial for developing a strong sense of self-authenticity and cultural identity. After all, life is a constant evolution.

Self-Awareness

It's crucial to gain a deeper awareness of ourselves if we want to practice self-authenticity and comprehend our own cultural identities. Examining several facets of our lives, such as our views, values, emotions, and relationships, is part of this.

We can discover more about who we are as people and begin to strengthen our connection to our cultural identity by looking at the aspects of our lives that define us.

Embracing Change

We need to be open to changes in the environment we live in as well as to changes within ourselves. This might entail accepting new ideologies or cultures that are different from our own, as doing so might open our eyes to fresh viewpoints and encourage us to further explore our own cultural identities.

## Connecting to Your Cultural Origins Has its Advantages.

You might not be aware of it, but maintaining a connection to your cultural background can be very beneficial.

- Pride and a Feeling of Belonging

Discovering your own culture is a wonderful way to feel proud of and at home in the world. Even if the group is merely virtual, having a sense of purpose and belonging can be beneficial. By staying connected to your culture, you can also learn new perspectives on life while drawing on the knowledge of your ancestors and previous generations. These elements could combine to form a solid feeling of identity that could then be used in day-to-day activities.

- Value Divergent Points of View

We can benefit from other people's opinions and cherish them in our own lives when we maintain a connection to our cultural roots. We begin to appreciate how each culture has its own distinct values, conventions, and rituals that have been passed down through the years as well as our growing openness to cultural differences. This also increases our appreciation for diversity.

- Boosted Self-Assurance

We will experience an increase in our self-confidence as well as better connections with others - both personally and professionally - if we express our actual selves truthfully, without fear or judgment. When we are sure of who we are and where we came from, we can stand tall and proud in any circumstance because we know that our truth will help us overcome any difficulties or obstacles that may come our way.

- Knowing Your Family and Traditions

Understanding your cultural roots will help you better comprehend the traditions and customs of your family. This can help you have a deeper understanding of your family's history and improve relations with your kin.

Developing a broader knowledge and understanding of other cultures can be accomplished by learning about your own cultural background. This can make you more understanding and accepting of other people, which is crucial in today's diverse culture.

- Professional Benefits

Understanding several cultures and languages may be a big plus in many professions. This is often the case in industries like business, politics, and diplomacy.

- Language Skills

Maintaining a connection to your cultural roots can help you pick up a new language or get better at one you already know. This can be helpful for both personal development and more pragmatic reasons like family communication, travel, or work chances.

- Culture Preservation

You can support the preservation of your culture and customs by developing a connection to your cultural roots. This is particularly crucial for cultures that may be at risk of disappearing or becoming diluted.

- Access to Networks and Resources

Maintaining a connection to your cultural roots can provide you access to networks and resources in your community. This can include tools that could be useful to you on the social, professional, and educational fronts.

- Feeling of adventure

Investigating your cultural roots may be a thrilling and enjoyable adventure. It can entail seeing and experiencing places you have never been before, tasting new foods, picking up new dances or musical instruments, and making new friends.

- Enhanced Creativity

You could find more inspiration for creative projects by connecting to your cultural roots. Writing, painting, music, and other forms of expression influenced by your cultural history fall under this category.

**Difficulties of Staying True to Yourself in a Multicultural Environment.**

It can be difficult to develop a feeling of cultural identity and self-authenticity, particularly while residing in a multi-cultural setting. Finding your own place in the world might be difficult because there are so many different cultures and religions coexisting there.

Here are some pointers to help you create your cultural identity and discover your personal authenticity while residing in a multicultural environment:

- Take the time to research your ancestry. Discuss your ancestry with your family members or try looking into your relatives' origins online or traveling to locations associated with those origins.

- Have an open mind regarding the cultures in your neighbourhood. To better understand other people's perspectives and cultures, read books and watch movies that tell stories from many cultures.

- Instead of fearing or avoiding diversity, embrace it as something that draws us closer together. Understanding that everyone is bonded by a common humanity might be facilitated by accepting others as members of the same multicultural world.

- Spend some time getting to know people from other cultures and ask them about their own experiences growing up in that culture. This will give you an understanding of the distinctive values that distinguish various societies, as well as how those values have influenced the people in those societies.

- Embrace variety and surround yourself with supportive individuals who can help you through difficult times, such as teachers, counsellors, or mentors who have knowledge of intercultural interactions and an appreciation for various viewpoints. You'll be able to get a deeper knowledge of how culture impacts our identities and how it can be used as a tool for personal growth in times of transition or crisis by surrounding yourself with various individuals and interacting with folks from different backgrounds. We can learn more about ourselves by being open-minded about many facets of culture, even those that are distinct from our own ancestry and experiences.

## Identifying Oneself in Communities.

Communities are another place where self-authenticity and cultural identity can be found. People in a community are able to discover and identify commonalities that can positively form their identities through shared experiences, values, and beliefs. Communities give people a place to go in search of self-discovery-promoting connections, understanding, and support.

- Finding Commonalities

Through recognizing parallels with others, we can develop a greater knowledge of who we are and what it means to be true to ourselves. When forging closer bonds with those around us, we can examine and test our beliefs, sentiments, and ideals. Also, by spotting similarities among community members, each person is able to grow in self-awareness, which ultimately results in the affirmation of cultural identity.

- Cultural Interaction

Communities serve as centres for cross-cultural interaction, which influences how authentically a person develops. People are exposed to various ways of life as they interact with various customs and traditions within the community.

This exposure inspires them to unlearn old thought or behaviour patterns in order to broaden their horizons, which in turn enables them to incorporate more ideas into their own lives and push the development of their identity beyond its predetermined boundaries.

Working together towards harmony allows people from all walks of life to gain a stronger footing in their exploration of self-authenticity in the context of cultural identity, whether it be through the sharing of common goals and aspirations among community members or the introduction of new perspectives that challenge pre-existing personal beliefs.

# Chapter Ten

## SELF AUTHENTICITY IN RELATIONSHIPS

How frequently do you stop and think, "Am I being my authentic self?" We are all aware that maintaining relationships, whether platonic or romantic, may be labour-intensive. But how much of ourselves ought to we be prepared to part with? It's critical to keep in mind that maintaining honest relationships is essential. Authenticity can strengthen bonds with our loved ones and aid in our personal development. But how can we be certain we're being authentic?

We'll look at the drawbacks and advantages of self-authenticity in relationships in this chapter. Also, we'll examine what it means to be self-authentic and discuss strategies you may employ to be true to who you are while maintaining deep relationships with the people in your life.

## Advantages and Disadvantages of Self Authenticity in Relationships

The benefits and drawbacks of self-authenticity in relationships are as follows:

## Advantages

- Increases Trust: Being genuine in a relationship increases trust between the two of you. You are demonstrating your integrity and openness, which might result in a stronger and deeper connection.

- Encourages Growth: Being genuine allows you to advance both as a relationship and as a person. Honest communication allows you to discover more about yourself and your spouse, which can help you both advance and evolve.

- Improves Emotional Intimacy: Being authentic in a relationship allows you to share your innermost thoughts and feelings with your spouse, which fosters emotional intimacy. A relationship that is more satisfying can result from this emotional connection.

- Reduces Resentment: Being authentic means that you are not hiding your emotions or trying to be someone you're not. This lessens the possibility of long-term resentment accumulation, which can harm a relationship.

- Improved Communication: Self-authenticity encourages both partners to express their needs and desires in an open and honest manner, which enhances communication in relationships. As a result, talks become more meaningful and mutual understanding increases.

- Increased Intimacy: When both partners are genuine, a secure and dependable environment is created in which they can be vulnerable with one another. This promotes a stronger emotional bond and increased closeness.

- Improved Self-Esteem: Being honest means not attempting to impress other people or pretending to be someone you're not. This leads to more self-esteem and self-confidence, which can improve the quality of your relationship.

- Increased Satisfaction: Couples who are authentically themselves are more likely to enjoy a meaningful and successful relationship. Their insistence on upholding their principles and demands can result in greater satisfaction and contentment.

## Disadvantages

- Conflict: Being honest in a relationship can occasionally cause conflict. There may not always be agreement between couples if they hold different values or ideas, which can lead to conflict.

- Rejection: Being real puts you at risk of having your lover reject you. It can be hurtful if your partner does not accept you for who you are if they do not share your values or ideas.

- Being genuine can occasionally be uncomfortable, especially if you are sharing an opinion that you passionately hold. This might lead to awkward or uncomfortable circumstances in your relationship.

- Being vulnerable is necessary for authenticity, which can be frightening. You are putting yourself in a vulnerable position where your partner can harm you or reject you, which can be challenging to bear.

- Tension can be produced in a relationship when one person is genuine and the other is not. As a result of their partner's lack of honesty or openness, the real partner could experience frustration or resentment.

- May be Overwhelming: Being honest can be overwhelming, especially if you are expressing strong emotions or tackling challenging topics. Working through this can be difficult for both couples and may take some time.

- May Cause Misunderstandings: Being sincere can occasionally cause miscommunication between spouses since they may interpret one another's emotions and thoughts differently. This could cause misunderstandings or uncertainty in the couple's relationship.

- Emotional intelligence is necessary since being real demands the ability to communicate your thoughts and feelings in a polite and straightforward manner. Some people may find this difficult, therefore practice and self-awareness may be necessary.

**Addressing Trust and Fear Problems.**

What exactly does the proverb "It's better to have loved and lost than never to have loved at all" mean? It entails being completely honest and shameless in relationships. You must go past any trust difficulties you may have accrued through time to accomplish this.

Trust problems may result from past relationships or even from interactions with close relatives, friends, or other family members. But in the end, being willing to trust your partner and the connection despite any prior experiences is the only way to reach self-authenticity in a relationship. You can start by being truthful with your partner and yourself about the reasons you might mistrust people to aid in this. To start opening up and communicating your genuine feelings with your spouse, you can also work on yourself and concentrate on accepting vulnerability, which involves taking chances in relationships.

Finally, keep in mind that upholding trust does not include disregarding warning signs or failing to set boundaries. An ideal relationship should strike a balance between mutual respect, free-flowing communication, and awareness of each other's needs.

Self-Respect and Vulnerability in Balance

Self-authenticity, at its foundation, calls for a sound balance between self-respect and vulnerability. Too much self-respect prevents you from being open and vulnerable with your lover. Nevertheless, if you're too open to attack, you might not be able to defend yourself. For true self-authenticity in relationships, striking a balance is crucial.

The following advice can help you achieve that balance:

- Don't be hesitant to share your thoughts or disagree with your partner because you respect yourself and your right to them. This enables you to respect yourself and your values while yet being real.
- Be truthful to yourself. When communicating with others, be open and truthful about your emotions and thoughts. Be conscious of the emotions that are motivating you, such as fear, wrath, guilt, or humiliation, and attempt to get rid of them before interacting with others.
- Open communication is crucial. You should tell your partner how you truly feel without fear of being judged or turned away. Say it out loud and discuss it with your partner if anything is upsetting you or if it makes you feel uneasy.
- We can create a place for self-authenticity that promotes trust in the relationship by striking a balance between self-respect and vulnerability in interpersonal interactions. We will ultimately have more satisfying relationships with both ourselves and others if we honour both sides of who we are!

## Getting Yourself Seen and Heard.

True self-authenticity in relationships is the capacity to be seen and heard. It involves being sincere with both you and other people to foster an atmosphere of respect, trust, and mutual understanding. It's about letting go of fear and judgment so that you can be seen for who you truly are.

What is your process then? Here are some recommendations on how to establish a safe space for yourself and others to be authentic:

- Say what you mean!

You must communicate honestly about your feelings and views in partnerships. Don't keep things within or assume what the other person could be thinking. Open communication between you both promotes a higher level of trust.

- Listen carefully!

To fully comprehend another person's viewpoint, it is crucial to listen intently. Pay attention to what they are saying and refrain from inserting your own opinions or presumptions. That calls for tolerance, compassion, and attentive listening without prejudice or judgment.

- Have an open mind!

Even though you don't have to agree on everything, it's crucial to keep an open mind when speaking to one another. This calls for putting aside any preconceived assumptions that can colour your perception of the other person and giving them the freedom to express their thoughts or feelings without fear of receiving any form of personal criticism.

In relationships, self-authenticity is essential to fostering an atmosphere of mutual respect, understanding, and trust where both parties can feel free to be who they truly are without worrying about being judged.

How to maintain self-authenticity in relationships

It's essential to keep your self-authenticity in relationships if you want to stay true to yourself and enjoy your interactions with others. These are some strategies for preserving your self-authenticity in relationships:

- Understand who you are, what you value, and what you want from life by taking the time to get to know yourself. It is simpler to detect when your needs and ideals are not being met in a relationship when you have a strong sense of who you are.
- Openly and honestly express yourself; be courteous and caring while doing so. Talk about your feelings, thoughts, and worries with your partner, and urge them to do the same. Passive-aggressive behaviour and lying about your genuine emotions should be avoided as they might cause resentment and misconceptions.
- Establish boundaries: Retaining one's self-authenticity in relationships requires boundaries. Communicate your boundaries to your partner and be clear about what you are and are not comfortable with. You should also respect your partner's boundaries.
- Be true to yourself: Don't sacrifice your principles to appease your partner or settle a dispute. Keep your commitments and be prepared to defend your principles when required.
- Be genuine: To impress or win over your lover, avoid trying to be someone you're not. Accept your peculiarities, passions, and character qualities, and let your spouse get to know the true you.
- Take care of your physical, emotional, and mental health by engaging in self-care. Being genuine to yourself in your relationships is more likely when you feel good about yourself.

- Consider your relationships and how they affect your sense of self by taking some time to think about them. Be prepared to adjust or end a relationship if required if you discover that it does not reflect your values or ambitions.

- Keep your dreams and goals in mind: Even in a partnership, it's critical to stay aware of your own unique objectives and aspirations. Even if your partner has different goals, make sure that yours are compatible with your values and that you are working towards them.

- Reflect on your ideas and feelings and how they connect to your relationship by engaging in self-reflection. This can aid in improving your self-awareness and your ability to interact with your spouse.

- Consider your gut instinct: Give attention to your intuition and gut instincts. It's crucial to identify and resolve any issues in your relationship if they arise rather than brushing them off.

- Do not sacrifice your own needs and desires to appease your partner or prevent disagreement. It's acceptable to disagree and hold opposing views if you do it in an open and respectful manner.

- Recognize your own tendencies and biases: Understand your personal prejudices and behavioural habits and how they may be affecting your relationships. This can make you more conscious of your own behaviour and improve your ability to communicate with your partner.

- Ask for help when you need it: If you're finding it difficult to be true to yourself in a relationship, don't be afraid to ask for help from friends, family, or a therapist. They can be a great source of wisdom and direction as you navigate your relationships.

Other pointers include:

- Even if it makes you uncomfortable at first, speak your truth.

- Recognize that the other individual might not feel or think the same as you do.

- Try to have an open discussion about various viewpoints rather than imposing your beliefs or opinions on other people.

- Be open to change, both yours and theirs, and develop constructive conflict management skills.

- Cooperate to achieve shared objectives that will bring out the best in one another.

- Recognize when it's appropriate to take a break or pause for thought before continuing a conversation and respect each other's personal boundaries.

You can create stronger bonds based on trust and honesty while still fostering your relationship's potential for growth through conflict resolution by remaining true to yourself while also taking into account another person's feelings and needs. This will ultimately bring the two of you along on the journey of life together as self-authentic individuals in love.

# Chapter Eleven

## SELF AUTHENTICITY IN CREATIVE PURSUITS

Self-authenticity in creative endeavours is the practice of remaining genuine to oneself while engaging in creative expression. It entails accessing one's deepest emotions, ideas, and experiences and using the creative process to express them in a sincere and self-aware way.

It's simple to get caught up in the trap of producing only a reflection of what we believe other people want to see or hear when engaging in creative endeavours. This may result in a lack of creativity and authenticity in our work, which would ultimately cause us to lose touch with both our audience and ourselves.

It's crucial to first have a clear knowledge of who we are as individuals and what we want to represent via our work in order to build self-authenticity in creative endeavours. To do this, we must take the time to consider our values, beliefs, and experiences and recognize the ways in which they influence our creative vision.

We can start using this energy for our creative endeavours once we have a firm understanding of who we truly are. This might entail experimenting with various mediums, methods, or aesthetics that fit our unique aesthetic and vision.

Being genuine to oneself requires a lot of courage, particularly when engaging in creative endeavours. Every one of us has a unique voice and story to share, and we are frequently prodded to go outside our comfort zones in an effort to advance in success or notoriety. Although this striving is admirable, it can also cause us to lose sight of what once made us special.

Self-authenticity is important if you want to have a real effect on any creative activity. What does it mean, though, exactly? How do you access your highest creative potential without losing the unique spark that makes you very uniquely you?

## The Value of Acceptance of Oneself

Self-acceptance is among the most crucial principles for creative endeavours. We can be our own worst critics all too frequently, fixating on the shortcomings and flaws in our work or even in ourselves. The truth is that accepting constructive criticism from others while also being able to accept yourself for who you are is necessary for change and growth.

It's critical to value yourself and keep in mind that making mistakes is perfectly normal; otherwise, there would be no possibility for improvement or personal development. It also supports the development of a creative and resilient environment to concentrate on positive self-talk rather than self-criticism.

Celebrating your accomplishments and proactively looking for opportunities to advance in your area are also important aspects of self-authenticity. Recognizing your accomplishments even for a brief period each day can help improve your confidence and keep things in perspective when difficult situations come.

**Investigating Personal Identity for Creative Development**

Your self-identity is critical when it comes to achieving success in creative endeavours. You must be at ease with who you are and comprehend the source of your passion and drive to create in an honest way.

Think for a moment on the source of your inspiration. Is it a thought or a dream? Is it influenced by things or occurrences that have personally occurred to you? These inquiries can direct your talents toward the right areas and reveal hidden sources of creativity.

Developing a strong sense of self-awareness can also assist in defending your creative interests against exploitation by other forces. Knowing who you are and what is most important to you makes it simpler to stay true to yourself even in the face of pressure or criticism from others.

In the end, knowing and accepting who you are only serves to inspire your creativity. It may even be the secret to achieving real success in the endeavour that ignites your passion.

How to Boost Your Self-Confidence

With creative endeavours, it can be difficult to find self-authenticity, especially if you lack confidence. Be at ease, though! There are actions you can perform to boost your self-assurance and security as an artist.

- Recognize What You Can Give

Prior to beginning to share your abilities with the world, it's critical to understand what makes you special. Explore what makes your creative abilities stand out from the rest and make a list of your strengths and limitations. Think about how your upbringing, life events, and morals have influenced your artistic style. Knowing your unique qualities will help you accentuate them when presenting your work to others.

- Embrace the Helpful Individuals in Your Life

You need a lot of energy and confidence to express yourself creatively, therefore it's crucial to establish connections with individuals who encourage and support your artistic development. Make connections with individuals who share your interests and hobbies so that you may have meaningful discussions about art, creativity, ideas, and inspiration. This will not only boost your self-confidence but also stimulate the creation of fresh creativity!

- Take Back the Creative Space

To access creative ideas and increase confidence, it is essential to create a relaxing environment. Whatever works best for you, reclaiming your creative space could entail designating a space in your home entirely for artistic pursuits or choosing a tranquil outdoor location. When engaged in creative activities, make sure there are no interruptions present so that nothing detracts from the voyage of self-discovery through artmaking.

Making Trusting Connections With the Creative Process

Developing a trustworthy relationship with the creative process is essential to being self-authentic in your creative endeavours. After all, it's that faith that encourages you to go on adventures and learn new things. Although it can be challenging to understand, the following advice will get you started:

- Make mistakes without fear of reprisal.

It's a terrific method to keep your feet firmly planted in the present when you accept and make mistakes without passing judgment. You can be receptive to the chance of learning something new by doing this.

- Accept curiosity.

We can explore the unfamiliar and keep our creative processes active by cultivating our curiosity. Also, it might provide a welcome short-term diversion from anxious or stressful periods experienced while working on a project.

- Get rid of perfectionism.

To foster authenticity, letting go of perfectionism is a crucial first step. When we let go of our need to be perfect or win others' approval, we can create freely and authentically.

You can develop the self-awareness required for partaking in self-authentic creative endeavours by developing a trusting relationship with your creative process. By doing this, we are inspired to take chances, explore uncharted territory, and overcome our fear of making mistakes, which eventually helps us discover the truth in our work.

- Honest Representation of Expression

Being true to yourself is the best course of action when it comes to creative endeavours and self-expression. Being honest with yourself is crucial because it enables you to express who you are authentically rather than what you think other people want you to be.

- Trying to Be More Open

Being open to your own ideas and emotions, especially when it's difficult, is the first step toward authenticity. Being at ease in the ambiguous spaces of uncertainty encourages self-expression. No matter how difficult it may be to convey your sentiments, you shouldn't ever feel ashamed or embarrassed about them.

- Overcoming the voices in your head

We all occasionally struggle with negative thoughts that tell us untrue stories about our qualifications or worth. To transcend these voices and discover a source of healing, it is critical to acknowledge them for what they are and use creative endeavours to communicate how they make you feel.

- Redirecting Your Focus

Try shifting your emphasis away from outside expectations or demands and back toward your own experience—your thoughts, ideas, interests, beliefs, and emotions—in order to truly embrace authenticity in creativity. This will assist you in knowing your own priorities and the most effective ways to communicate in a way that makes you feel empowered.

**Obtaining Inspiration Both Internally and Outside.**

It might be beneficial to both seek within and outside of yourself for inspiration when you're trying to be creative. When looking for inspiration, it's crucial to draw from both the inside and outside environment.

- Seeing Inward

As you examine yourself, you examine the thoughts, emotions, and experiences that have shaped who you are. This can include past experiences, influences, or any other major event in your life. Considering issues such as "What motivates me?" What have I learned, for example? can assist in revealing characteristics of oneself that may provide insight into what motivates one.

- Looking Outside for Inspiration

The people in your life or other creative works can serve as external inspiration sources. You could get inspiration from your favourite novels, movies, poetry, and works of art, or even use them as a source of information while beginning a new endeavour. The final product must be authentically you and not just a carbon duplicate of someone else's work, even though these inspirations may be useful for igniting a fresh concept.

At the end of the day, it's crucial to be your most real self when developing and pursuing any creative activity. We give ourselves the best chance for increased potential, progress, and success when we set aside other people's expectations and work on something that stimulates and excites us.

It's critical to keep in mind that there is no one-size-fits-all method for exercising creativity and self-expression, and what works for one individual might not work for you. Instead, be faithful to your own preferences, values, and aspirations and let them direct your work.

You can produce something that is wholly representative of who you are by embracing your authentic self and making it the centre of everything you do. As a result, you will experience a strong sense of pride, joy, and fulfilment.

# There You Have It!

---

As we come to the end of our journey towards self-authenticity, it's worth noting that the road to true self-discovery isn't always smooth sailing. But then again, where's the fun in smooth sailing? It's the rough waters and high waves that make for the most exciting adventures, after all. And the adventure of self-discovery is no exception.

So, what have we learned? We've learned that being authentic means being true to yourself, no matter what others may think or say. It means taking risks, exploring your innermost thoughts and desires, and staying true to your values and beliefs. It's a journey of self-discovery that requires patience, courage, and a willingness to embrace the unknown.

But the rewards of self-authenticity are worth the effort. When you're living authentically, you'll feel a sense of peace and contentment that comes from knowing you're living your best life. You'll have stronger, more meaningful relationships with the people around you. And you'll be a happier, more fulfilled person overall.

So, as we close this chapter on self-authenticity, I challenge you to take a step back and reflect on your own journey! Have you been living authentically? Have you been true to yourself, even when it's been hard? If not, don't worry — it's never too late to start. Embrace the adventure of self-discovery and remember that the rough waters make for the most exciting ride. Bon voyage!